T0319235

Mau Mau, the Revolutionary, Anti-Imperialist Force from Kenya

1948-63

Kenya Resists No. 1

Selection from Shiraz Durrani's Kenya's War of Independence: Mau Mau and its Legacy of Resistance to Colonialism and Imperialism, 1948-1990 (2018, Nairobi: Vita Books).

And

Book Review by Willy Mutunga: MacArthur, J. (Ed) Dedan Kimathi on Trial. Athens, Ohio: Ohio University Press, 2017.

Kenya Resists
No. 1 (2018)

VITA BOOKS

P.O Box 62501-00200

Nairobi. Kenya

http://vitabooks.co.uk

info.vitabkske@gmail.com; info@vitabooks.co.uk

Series: Kenya Resists No.1 2018

Distributed Worldwide by:

African Books Collective

PO BOX 721

Oxford, OX1 9EN

orders@africanbookscollective.com

www.africanbookscollective.com

ISBN 978-9966-804-02-0 (Paper)

ISBN 978-9966-1890-8-0 (eBook)

**Dedicated to
Dedan Kimathi, General Kago
and all those who fought for Kenya's
independence.**

Contents

PART 1

Preface to the Series, Kenya Resists

Looking Back to Fight Forward

People need to know their history in order to understand their past and present and chart out the desired outcomes for the future – in the tradition of "Looking back to fight forward". But in a class divided society where people do not have the power to keep their history alive, those who do have power manipulate, distort and hide historical facts and interpret history from their class perspective. They thus satisfy their class interests against the interest of working people.

Kenya won independence after a bloody confrontation with Britain after the sacrifices of lives, limbs, land and property of hundreds of thousands – not to mention collective punishments, unpaid slave labour and concentration camps for millions. The sacrifices affected not only the generation involved in the war, but future generations as well. Those who fought in various ways for independence saw a minority elite, groomed under the watchful eye of imperialism, take all the power and benefits of independence.

Among the losses that working people suffered was the control over their history. Their oral histories were allowed to die with the death of those involved – directly or indirectly – in the War of Independence. Imperialism took charge of interpreting the anti-colonial, anti-imperialist war from their perspective, turning our heroes into villains and our enemies into heroes. Their version of history hid the achievements of people who refused to live on their knees and heaped praise on the homeguards, the protectors of imperialist interest.

Few school textbooks depicting the reality of the war of independence exist after more than 50 years of independence; schools do not teach working class history of Kenya and radical trade unions do not feature in any curriculum – or in national consciousness. Bookshops and public libraries have poor collections on Kenyan history and even these do not show the anti-imperialist and class perspectives of the war of independence. Attempts by progressive historians and writers to address this imbalance by documenting people's perspective of Kenya's history have been ruthlessly stopped by the ruling elites directly or by intimidation. Kenya has seen over 50 years of lies, distortions, manipulation of history and hiding the loot of national wealth by the elite and their imperialist masters. And, at the same time, over 50 years of resistance to the lies, distortions, manipulation of history and hiding the loot of national wealth by working people is also hidden by the elite.

It is in this context that Vita Books has published a number of books on the progressive history of the working class and its class allies. These include titles such as *Never be Silent*, *Makhan Singh* and *Liberating Minds* (see further details of these books on the last pages of this handbook or at http:vitabooks.co.uk). While the earlier books were published in London out of necessity, the situation changed with the relocation of the publisher to Kenya in 2016-17. The latest book – *Kenya's War of Independence* - was launched in February 2018 in Nairobi. Yet another important step by Vita Books is in addressing not only the content of its books, but to meet the needs of working people in terms of the *form* of such publications. It was felt that working people may not have time or resources to read large titles such as *Kenya's War of Independence* with its 448 pages covering over 40 years of Kenya's history.

Vita Books is therefore pleased to announce the launch of this new Series of handbooks under the title *Kenya Resists*. The new Series

8

covers different aspects of the resistance by people of Kenya to colonialism and imperialism. The readings are reproduced from published books, unpublished reports, research and oral or visual testimonies. Each title carries references on its particular topic to encourage readers to read and study further on these topics.

The Series aims to provide an insight into the history of resistance by people of Kenya. The Series focuses on specific aspects of resistance before and after independence, specifically Mau Mau, trade unions peasants and nationalities. Wherever appropriate and possible, Vita Books will translate the Series into Kiswahili or relevant nationality languages so as to reach the intended audiences. In this way the Series will make historical material accessible to its intended readers.

The first titles in the Series has been taken from Shiraz Durrani's book, *Kenya's War of Independence, Mau Mau and its Legacy of Resistance to Colonialism and Imperialism, 1948-1990* (2018, Nairobi: Vita Books). Some relevant material from earlier publications is also added when appropriate. The first three titles to be published in the Series in 2018 are:

1. Mau Mau, the Revolutionary, Anti-Imperialist Force from Kenya 1948-63

2. Trade Unions and Kenya's War of Independence. Also includes *Reflections on the Revolutionary Legacy of Makhan Singh*. Reproduced from: Durrani, Shiraz (Ed.) 2015: Makhan Singh: A Revolutionary Kenyan Trade Unionist. Nairobi: Vita Books.

3. People's Resistance to Colonialism and Imperialism in Kenya (includes Somali, Kamba, Maasai and South Asian Kenyans, women, peasants, workers and students). It also

includes presentations from the event to commemorate the revolutionary work of Shujaa Karimi Nduthu held on March 24, 2018 in Nairobi at the Professional Centre.

The choice of these three topics for the new Series is not accidental. The three aspects – Mau Mau, trade unions and nationalities – make up the three pillars of resistance against the British forces. Durrani (2018) explains the significance of the three:

Thus in essence, the War of Independence was a movement built on three pillars of resistance to colonialism and imperialism. These can be seen as Mau Mau (which included the armed and people's forces with participants from the other two pillars), the trade union movement (including all organised workers in towns and rural areas) and the people's forces consisting of peasants, national and nationality political and social organisations from across the country who supported the War of Independence in different ways, not necessarily always supporting armed resistance. (p.46).

It is necessary to see the unity of the above three forces in order to understand the process of resistance that finally forced colonialism from Kenya. A similar unity will be necessary in the struggle against imperialism and the comprador regime today.

Finally a word about the title of the Series, *Kenya Resists*. Resistance, as understood here, is resistance to colonialism, imperialism as well as to the capture of the Kenyan state by comprador forces after independence with the active connivance of imperialism. The working people of Kenya will certainly need to look back at their history in order to liberate themselves from the grip of imperialism. So we echo Bertold Brecht's call, "Reach for the book, it is a weapon" ([1]) – a weapon to preserve and sustain life, no less.

---

1   (1) Available at: https://www.goodreads.com/author/quotes/26853.Bertolt_Brecht

Preface to Kenya Resists No. 1

Mau Mau, the Revolutionary Force from Kenya Challenges Colonialism and Imperialism

Very few countries in the world hide or obscure the significance of their most important historical achievements. Kenya has managed to do so without any regrets or even a thought about historical accuracy in connection with Mau Mau. Imagine if the Russian and Chinese Revolutions were similarly ignored. That would just not happen. Yet Kenya shies away from Mau Mau, which, with the Algerian War of Independence and the Maji Maji resistance movement in Tanganyika, among others, was one of the most significant achievements in African – indeed, world – history.

The reason for this underplay of the achievement of Mau Mau in Kenya is not difficult to understand. Two factors explain this. First, the government that came to power at independence was not only not part of the Mau Mau movement which fought for land and freedom for working people, but actively opposed it. It sought – and was given by the departing colonial power – state power, land and freedom for its class, thereby sidelining the radical resistance movement and its activists. This elite then used its state power to ensure that the nation forgets its radical history which would have alerted future generations to the theft of their inheritance and country.

The above fact then influences the second factor sidelining Mau Mau: that there are two Kenyas and it is the elite ruling class in power which seeks to silence the voice of Mau Mau and those who support it today. But theirs is not the only voice in Kenya. The voice of the majority

[Accessed: 16-10-17].

of working people, silenced by official order, is nevertheless present underground. The majority, especially the young, remain hungry for the history, the achievements and an appropriate evaluation of Mau Mau from a working class perspective. Their resistance to everything represented by the corrupt ruling elite is in daily evidence. The ruling class can stay in power only by its acts since independence of massacres, jailing and daily killings of Kenyan youth by police, GSU and shadowy thugs sponsored by the elite.

This book provides essential facts about Mau Mau. It seeks to give voice to the Mau Mau resistance fighters who were assassinated or sidelined by the ruling class with the active participation of imperialists who benefited from the rule by this minority elite. It is aimed at young people who were born after independence and who have been deprived of their historical heritage; it is also a tribute to those who played a part in the war of independence and in Mau Mau without whose contribution independence would have remained a dream. So we echo Bertold Brecht's call, "Reach for the book, it is a weapon"[2] – a weapon to preserve and sustain life, no less.

Shiraz Durrani
London
12-03-2018

---

2 . Available at: https://www.goodreads.com/author/quotes/26853.Bertolt_Brecht [Accessed: 16-10-17].

PART 1 MAU MAU, 1948-1960

> The worst illiterate is the political illiterate, he doesn't hear, doesn't speak, nor participates in the political events. He doesn't know the cost of life, the price of the bean, of the fish, of the flour, of the rent, of the shoes and of the medicine, all depends on political decisions. The political illiterate is so stupid that he is proud and swells his chest saying that he hates politics. The imbecile doesn't know that, from his political ignorance is born the prostitute, the abandoned child, and the worst thieves of all, the bad politician, corrupted and flunky of the national and multinational companies. - Bertolt Brecht [3]

Mau Mau, The Revolutionary Force

Preparations for Armed Struggle

Soon after the Second World Imperialist War, the hopes of peaceful removal of colonialism from Kenya began to fade. The revolutionary line of armed, organised people's war began to emerge by around 1948. The lessons of the past struggles were clear to the advanced workers: the contradiction between colonialism and imperialism could not be resolved without an organised, armed confrontation. This realisation began to be put into practice gradually as the subjective and objective conditions developed. It was becoming clear that in the meantime, intense working class struggles under Makhan Singh and Fred Kubai had developed ideas and experiences of working class struggles and organisations that added to the anti-capitalist arsenal at the disposal of working people. At the same time, social and political activists had decided that the formation of a new organisation was necessary to meet new challenges of fighting colonialism. Thus was born Mau Mau. The name came later, but its organisation, its ideology, its vision, its strategies were all decided by the conditions of the time in the struggle against a foreign power that had captured people's land, people's labour, the country's resources and

---

3 Available at: https://www.goodreads.com/author/quotes/26853.Bertolt_Brecht [Accessed: 16-10-17].

had created an unequal and unjust system to maintain their power, to exploit, to oppress and to govern.

The requirement at the beginning was to organise secretly when the need for unity was paramount among the active combatants. One of the ways of achieving unity was to organise an oath for active fighters. Thus, thousands of people began to take the unity oath for Uhuru. By the end of 1950, over one hundred and forty had been prosecuted in colonial courts on charges related to oath taking. The colonial Government realised the strength behind the new organisation and banned 'Mau Mau' on August 12, 1950. Singh (1969) explains the aims and organisation of Mau Mau in those early days thus:

> A major development in the period following the general strike (of May, 1950) was the rapid progress of a secret mass organisation. The organisation, which previously had been in existence for some time, could be joined by persons of any (Kenyan nationality) who took an oath according to their customs, traditions and beliefs, pledging themselves to secrecy, dedication and sacrifice for the cause of land and freedom of Kenya. The aim of the Uhuru-oath organisation was to unite and mobilise the African people of Kenya in the struggle for independence and to resort to armed struggle against the colonialists if and when it became obvious to the organisation that there was no other way of achieving independence of Kenya.

> In the course of some court cases, which took place during and after June, 1950, the Uhuru-oath organisation began to be called Mau Mau. Later, when the organisation had to resort to armed struggle against the colonialists it began to be called the Kenya Land and Freedom Army.

There was a period of transition on the political front as people began to realise that the moderate approach of peaceful petitions to gain rights and justice was not likely to lead to independence and the settlement of land and freedom issues. Gachihi (1968) indicates the role of the trade union movement in making this transition to armed resistance possible:

The change of policy from petitioning to violence came with a militant, younger and uncompromising leadership that had begun to emerge in the ranks of KAU, having realized the futility of peaceful negotiations. This corresponded with the ban imposed on trade union activities in 1950 after a general strike. Many staunch trade unionists found in KAU a vehicle with which to vent their energy and militant attitude formerly exercised in trade union activities. They revived KAU's Nairobi branch and its activities countrywide. From this there developed a very intricate relationship between KAU and Mau Mau. An important development in the party occurred with these new and militant supporters who called not just vaguely for 'Independence', but "Independence now!" Three notable trade unionists-namely Fred Kubai, Bildad Kaggia and J. M. Mungai - stood out and were easily chosen to lead the Nairobi Branch of KAU with Kubai as the Chairman, Mungai as the Vice Chairman and B. Kaggia as its Secretary. These men were to bring with them into KAU's new phase the discipline and trade union tactics that they were so familiar with. Violence, long simmering in African circles, began to find a new venue in KAU. Clandestine oathing ceremonies that had started in the Rift Valley, where the squatters had sharply felt the effects of colonial rule, began to spread in Nairobi and its environs, taking an increasingly important role in the union's main branch in Nairobi. This oath was different in the sense that it was different in form and context from the traditional oaths or those taken by the KCA members. In Olenguruone, this "new" oath called for "freedom" and participants were thoroughly lectured on the purpose and meaning of the oath. KAU militants aimed at harnessing all oathing activities and, as a first step, intensifying it in the African locations in Nairobi and its environs. The decision by F. Kubai and Mungai to take the oath and to bring some of their 'most trusted associates' was significant in the development of the Mau Mau in that from this group was to be formed the 'Action group'. The so-called "trusted associates" were at first ten in number. Later 24 trade unionists joined and they all saw the founding of the Action Group. With the formation of this group, one begins to see organized violence and acts of terrorism. Particular groups of people were oathed and commissioned to carry out particular tasks. Taxi men, for example, were used for ferrying people to and from oathing places. Arms collection began to be accelerated and according to F. Kubai, even Nairobi prostitutes had their role to play. He says, "Some four hundred prostitutes from Nairobi African areas of Pumwani and Eastleigh were oathed and told to collect whatever information would help the movement.

It will be seen that workers not only provided the leadership of this new, radical movement but were also in the forefront of providing active support to the movement. Capitalism had created conditions for a mass dislocation of people who were left without adequate means of survival. From among those rose the *Anake a 40* organisation which was to play an important political role in the struggle for independence. Furedi (1973) provides a background of the organisation:

> The *Anake a 40* was founded by Dominic Gatu and a number of young, dissatisfied Nairobi Kikuyu. Its first members were the unemployed, petty traders, thieves, prostitutes and others of the lumpen proletariat of Nairobi. Many of the leaders were ex-soldiers and traders who felt that within the colonial system there was little scope for their skills and ambitions. Many of the leaders saw the 40 Age Group as the vanguard of the African nationalist movement. According to one of its leaders, '. . . we felt that K.A.U. was going too slow and that the only way to change things was through violence. This was why we started armed robberies. Most of the Africans in Nairobi were behind us and they would not inform the police of our activities.'

The organization established links with the trade union movement as well as with the radical wings of KAU. It "played a central role in the movement which the government called the Mau Mau" Furedi (1973) and established links with working class people in Nairobi as well as in the so-called Reserves created by colonialism. They continued to play an important role after the Declaration of Emergency, as Furedy 1973) records: "During the early part of 1953 their main activity was to supply ammunition, medical supplies and recruits for the fighters in the forest". Furedi (1973) concludes:

> They played a pivotal role in the organizing and financing of the 'Mau

Mau' throughout Kenya, and thus the role of the Nairobi populist movement in the nationalist struggle cannot be underestimated.

A study of the differing forms of organisation of Mau Mau reveals that changing conditions at different stages of the struggle gave rise to corresponding changes in the resistance organisation accompanied by a refinement of ideologies, which then resolved the particular problems of the day. Thus the organisation of the revolutionary movement was quite different in its early years (i.e. before October, 1952) from that which evolved after 1952, which again was different from that which emerged by 1955 and again by 1960.

In the early years, new cadres were recruited and given political education in preparation for the time when they would become fully active in resistance. Prospective members were placed under observation, then given the first oath, that of unity. They were then given specific tasks to test their commitment. At the same time, they were placed in an underground cell structure and assigned to work at a democratic level in legal organisations. Many of these became part of the Mau Mau intelligence-gathering network.

The task of military preparation was not being ignored even at the early stage, although the time for armed struggle was not considered ready yet. Many cadres were being given military training in the forests and the procurement of arms and ammunition was also going on. As early as 1948, arms were being captured from enemy forces and kept in readiness for the time when conditions made an armed struggle inevitable.

The particular form of organisation of Mau Mau during this period reflected existing conditions. A somewhat decentralised organisation was necessary so as to allow maximum security and room for building up leadership and organisational qualities among new recruits by allowing greater opportunity for local initiative. At the same time, it was still possible to operate without much harassment from the colonial armed forces, as they were not really aware of the extent of the preparations being made. Furedi (1989) looks at the transformation of the "loose network of militant activists" into Mau Mau when conditions required a stronger central organisation:

The transformation of a loose network of militant activists into the movement known as Mau Mau came through a process of experimentation and adaptation to the external environment. The breakdown of the uneasy alliance with the moderate wing of the KCA was a result of frustration with its lack of effectiveness. Since it appeared that the colonial government was in no mood to compromise, the militant option seemed the only way forward to the younger generations. The split with the moderate elements was consolidated through the establishment of separate committees of militant activists, an initiative that came from Nairobi. Their spread to the White Highlands in early 1950 indicated the close links forged with activists in Nairobi. Until that time the squatter movement had operated through area branches loosely linked together through the KCA. Now the formation of separate committees provided the organizational foundation for more militant forms of action.

It suited the colonial interests to ignore such organisational developments and continue its propaganda that Mau Mau was an "illegitimate, perverted force" (Furedi, 1989).

The War Begins

A new situation developed after 1947 under increasing activities by the trade union movement. There was a general strike in Mombasa on January 13, 1947 when over 15,000 workers took part and led to the formation of the African Workers Union, later renamed the African Workers' Federation. The strike "started with dock workers and railwaymen, and quickly spread to virtually all Africans including the houseboys and sugar workers at Ramisi on the mainland", according to Clayton and Savage (1974).

Following the Mombasa strike, workers in other parts of Kenya "came to the conclusion that unless they themselves went on strike, no notice would be taken of their demands" (Singh, 1969). There were strikes in Kisumu, Kisii, Mason, Luanda, Asembo Bay and other towns.

The colonial Government was fast losing its control over events and people. It reacted by arresting the trade union leaders. In 1951, the working class replied by staging a boycott of colonial buses and foreign beer in protest against colonial repression, supported by Mau Mau. Mau Mau forces began to attack traitors, Homeguards and other enemy targets. Fearing it would soon become totally ineffective, the colonial government declared a State of Emergency in October 1952, thus acknowledging its inability to govern without open military suppression. Immediately, about one hundred and eight political and trade union leaders were detained. British battalions poured into Kenya and the British ship *Kenya* docked at Mombasa. As Makhan Singh (1969) said: "A new chapter had begun. A new imperialist colonial war was now on against the people of Kenya".

Mau Mau had made some preparations for such an eventuality. It had already started early preparations for the armed stage of the struggle. It still had to adjust to this new situation and prepare for active resistance. It was no longer possible to be active in the above-ground movements. Although many of its activists had been detained, it had prepared for such an emergency. Every responsible cadre had a second in command who would take over the work if the former were detained. This enabled Mau Mau to continue its work in this new period. It is also true that to some extent, the Declaration of Emergency and the subsequent attacks on people forced many to become armed fighters and others to join people's forces. Many had no training for this new phase and this caused disruption to organisational structures and discipline in Mau Mau.

The military aspect became the principle one in this period. All activities were geared to serving this new demand. This included more urgent procurement of arms and ammunition; a new network of cadres to ensure the safe conduct of cadres and supplies to the newly established forest headquarters; the supply of intelligence on the strength and movement of enemy forces; acquisition of technicians and technologies to establish armament and other factories and facilities in the liberated areas in the city and in the forest headquarters; the establishment of underground hospitals for the treatment of wounded guerrillas. All these and other urgent tasks demanded a close-knit, efficient organisation. In addition, the presence of heavily armed enemy military occupation forces made it essential that security of cadres and organisation itself were given priority.

The changed situation resulted in organisational strengthening in Mau Mau. The basic level of organisation was via a network of small cells of just a few members who, for security reasons, did not know members of other cells or any members at higher levels. A number of such cells, represented by its leader, formed the next unit. A number of such units then formed a locality unit, which again sent representatives to the District Committees. At the head came the Central Committee, which oversaw the whole struggle through various committees.

In the meantime, there was a shift in the balance of power at an organisational level between the moderate KAU approach and the approach of radical groups influenced by involvement in trade union and other progressive activities. The radical groups took over the powerful Nairobi branch of KAU, but this was not happening only in the capital. It was fast turning into a national programme, as Furedi (1989) shows:

> Under grassroots pressure the KAU men were forced to take on a radical posture. In Elburgon and Thomson's Falls matters went further when the KAU branches were taken over by young militants in 1952 during the months leading up to the declaration of a State of Emergency. In these areas at least the very character of KAU had changed as the old leadership lost control over the organization it had created.

> The developments below would not have been possible without this radical transition in the organisation.

The Establishment of Liberated Territories

The years that followed the Declaration of Emergency by the colonial government saw dramatic changes in the political and military situation and the establishment of liberated territories by Mau Mau as seen in the following brief review. Barnett and Njama (1966) sum up the position by the first half of 1954:

> It was certainly true that after almost a year and a half of fighting, and with vastly superior weapons, the (Colonial) Government seemed no closer to defeating the insurgent forces. In fact, guerrilla

strength seemed to be growing, with Kenya Levellation Army units more active than ever in the reserve, a Nairobi Land and Freedom Army formed and very active, supplies flowing from the city into the forests, and Government apparently unable to launch a winning offensive against the guerrilla armies of Nyandarwa and Mt. Kenya

A report in the *Manchester Guardian*[4] revealed the extent of Mau Mau control, as seen by the British Establishment:

> In June 1953 things were going badly in Kenya. Parts of Kikuyuland were virtually Mau Mau republics, and the great majority of the Kikuyu were passive supporters of Mau Mau. The gangs in the forests of the Aberdares and Mount Kenya were living fairly comfortably. They were well supplied with food and clothing, with stolen arms and ammunitions, with women to tend for them, and with information of the movements of the security forces. They had effective communications by couriers with Nairobi. They were able to raid, murder and to pillage over most of Kikuyuland and into the surrounding settled areas. Nairobi was a hot-bed of Mau Mau. The greater part of the population of the city was intimidated, living in terror of the gangsters. Mau Mau were able to enforce a boycott of the buses, and on the smoking of cigarettes, and the drinking of beer.

So successful had Mau Mau been that large areas of land and people had been liberated from colonial rule. These included not only the forest bases in Nyandarwa and Mount Kenya which were "impregnable to the (colonial) army" (Odinga, 1968); there were semi-liberated rural areas in the settler farms and in the so called "reserves". In addition, there were liberated and semi-liberated areas in Nairobi itself, which was the centre of colonial rule in Kenya. Large parts of the city of Nairobi were under the rule of the guerrilla forces; others were controlled by the colonial army by day but were taken over by the Mau Mau by night.

The full extent of Mau Mau control in Nairobi became known to the colonial authorities towards the end of 1954 as the followings reports show:

---

4 Quoted from the Kenya Committee for Democratic Rights Press Briefings. 2-5-55.

A severe blow was struck at the Mau Mau movement by the destruction of their base in Nairobi during "Operation Anvil". Since then, Mau Mau leaders and organisers had been unable to send recruits, money, food, weapons and ammunition, and the information to the forest gangs and to those who belonged to the elaborate organisation in African Reserves and farming areas ... At times a large roving gang could still strike a severe blow.5

Another report indicated the infrastructure set up by Mau Mau in the liberated areas in the forests:

Reports so far received (as part of Operation Hammer) (reveal) the significant feature of the first phase has been the large number of hideouts found (in the Aberdare forests), some considerable size and many were skilfully constructed. One consisted of four huts capable of holding 80 men and with a piped water supply from a waterfall 30 yards away. [6]

The guerrilla forces established their own government in these liberated areas, controlled law and order in the interest of Kenyan people, ran an effective administration with its own legal system and a policy for financial control with its own taxes to finance the war effort. It was this tax levied in liberated and semi-liberated areas in the enemy territory that bought guns, ammunition, food and other supplies for the guerrilla army. It established hospitals as well as factories for the manufacture of armaments and other necessities such as clothing. Some details of Mau Mau infrastructures are recorded later in the book.

Mau Mau forces had liberated large areas even before the Declaration of Emergency; in fact this was one of the reasons why the colonial administration felt the need to declare the Emergency. This process of liberation was recorded in the Corfield Report (1960). It admitted that by August 1952 in large parts of Central Province, which was the primary battleground in that period leading up to independence, colonial law and law courts "had virtually ceased to exist". Their function had been taken over by the emerging Mau Mau administration, which established revolutionary justice for the workers

---

5 East African Standard, 15 October, 1954.
6 *The Times* (London), 14 January, 1955.

and peasants of Kenya and carried out sentences against colonial officers, saboteurs and other anti-people elements. Thus between May and October 1952 (before the Declaration of Emergency) fifty-nine Homeguard traitors, including the colonial Chief Waruhiu had been sentenced by the liberation courts and the sentences were carried out by the armed forces of the people.

As the armed struggle advanced after 1952, so did it increase the areas that were liberated by Mau Mau forces. They began to control large administrative machinery, which had jurisdiction over vast areas with hundreds of thousands of people over whose economy, welfare, education, health and security they were responsible. An official report (Great Britain. Colonial Office. Parliamentary Delegation to Kenya. Report, 1954) admitted the control established by Mau Mau:

> It is our view based upon all the evidence available to us, both from official and responsible unofficial sources, that the influence of Mau Mau in the Kikuyu area (i.e. the whole of Central Province and parts of Rift Valley and the Highlands), except in certain localities, has not declined; it has, on the contrary, increased; in this respect the situation has deteriorated and the danger of infection outside the Kikuyu area is now greater, not less, than it was at the beginning of the State of Emergency ... In Nairobi, the situation is both grave and acute. Mau Mau orders are carried out in the heart of the city, Mau Mau courts sit in judgement and their sentences are carried out. There is evidence that the revenues collected by (Mau Mau), which may be considerable are used for the purposes of bribery as well as for purchasing Mau Mau supplies ... There is also a passive resistance movement among Africans, an example of which is a bus boycott under which Africans have for several months boycotted European-owned buses.

In addition, Mau Mau's organisation, structures and influence had reached outside the borders of Kenya. Thus the Government of Tanganyika [now Tanzania] declared a state of emergency in North Tanganyika, and Kenyans from North Tanganyika and Zanzibar were deported in increasing numbers for fear of spreading ideas of liberation in these areas and to cut off the supply structures to Kenyan liberation forces. The Tanganyika government set up a detention centre at Urembo in Tanganyika for Kenyan detainees.[7] Some other details on the situation are also recorded by Kenya Committee's Press Extracts:

- The Tanganyika Government arrested and expelled Kenyans living in the Kilimanjaro area on the Kenya border.[8]

- Over 1500 Kikuyus arrested in northern Tanganyika – a Kenyan officer taking part in the arrests had already been sentenced [by Mau Mau] for the torture of captured Kikuyu[9]

- Tanganyika Government announces that Kikuyu women and children in the Northern Province – about 5000 in all – would be sent to new restricted areas in the colony.[10]

- The Tanganyika Government declares a state of emergency in the Northern Province. [11]

- 44 Wakamba were arrested in Tanganyika and returned to Kenya during a police round up in the Northern Province. [12]

- There were Mau Mau cells in Mombasa, Pemba, Zanzibar, and other coastal regions. In Tanzania, the movement [Mau Mau] succeeded in winning over hundreds of Kenyan migrant workers. Mau Mau cells were established mainly in northern and Tanga regions where the bulk of these Kenyan migrant labourers worked and resided. In their attempt to contain the spread of the anti-imperialist resistance in Uganda and Tanzania, the colonial authorities in both countries banned the Mau Mau Organisation and severe punishments were meted out to those who were suspected of being members. In Tanzania, a state of emergency was declared in the northern and Tanga regions and police and army were ordered to round up Gikuyu, Embu, Meru and

---

7   Kenya Committee. Press Extracts, Vol.1 (2 January, 1954), p. 49.
8   Kenya Committee. Press Extracts, Vol.1 (10 November, 1952), p. 14.
9   Kenya Committee. Press Extracts, Vol.1 (11 January, 1954), p. 49.
10 Kenya Committee. Press Extracts, Vol.1 (14 January, 1954), p.50.
11 Kenya Committee. Press Extracts, Vol.1 (14 January, 1954), p.50.
12 Kenya Committee. Press Extracts, Vol.1 (17 June, 1955), p. 142.

Kamba (GEMK) workers and put them in concentration camps. Thousands were arrested, tortured and then deported to Kenya where they were further brutalised and then sent to Manyani concentration camp. In Uganda, all the GEMK students attending Makerere University were arrested, interrogated and then deported to Kenya. The GEMK traders who had established business in Uganda were also subjected to the same brutality. Both colonies worked with the colonial regime in Kenya to fight the Mau Mau forces. They supplied the colonial Kenya government with intelligence, men and war material. [13]

· The Ethiopian intelligence is aware of what is going on in Kenya. Mau Mau and its causes are subjects about which they frequently ask questions. On the face of it there seems to be a parallel with their own mountain rebels, the Shiftas.[14]

· Mau Mau influence reached South Africa as well, as shown by a letter from A.J. Simpson who wrote: "I am on holiday in S. Africa where it is considered there is an underground movement by the natives to overthrow established Government throughout Africa and this is certainly the idea of Mau Mau". [15]

These facts, although well documented, remain outside general awareness about Mau Mau. It should be noted that military preparations had been taking place after the Second Imperialist World War and many military trainers of Mau Mau guerrillas were veterans of that war. Kabubi (2002), for instance, replies to the question *Tell us about your military training* thus:

I was, like all the Mau Mau guerrillas, trained by a World War II veteran. His name was Mbithi Manyuira. i was trained in the use of the 303 Enfield rifle, the Bren gun, and the Sten gun, and also in *gaturauhoro* -"a big gun to kill elephant."

13   Kinyatti (2008): The quote here and later from this source are taken from an
      early draft.
14   Manchester Guardian. 12 January, 1955.
15   Kenya Weekly News. 19 November, 1954.

Once again, the history of Mau Mau lacks details about its military preparations, trainers and gun and ammunition factories, which then leads to misunderstanding the armed resistance movement.

The Birth of Kenya Defence Council (1953)

After the declaration of a state of war (called the 'Emergency' by the colonial government) in October 1952,[16] the stage of armed resistance began in earnest. The guerrilla forces established their new military headquarters in the forests from where the armed battles were planned and executed. This military need was felt at the level of organisation as well. Many small and large guerrilla units had entered the forests and waged battles against the enemy in their local areas. Mau Mau recognised the need to co-ordinate the activities of these different fighting units and to form an umbrella military organisation that could control the overall strategy of warfare in the face of a well-armed and equipped enemy.

After about eight months of armed warfare, during which valuable military and guerrilla warfare experience had been gained, it was decided to call a representative meeting of the various units. The meeting was held in August 1953 near the Mwathe River and came to be known as the Mwathe Conference. After an exchange of ideas and long discussions, a decision was made to form the Kenya Defence Council as the highest military and political organ of the armed struggle. In keeping with the needs of the armed struggle, the Kenya Defence Council resolved the contradictions between a central authority and the need for local units to have a certain amount of autonomy so as to become more effective in the war situation. Thus, as Barnett and Njama (1966) say, while the Kenya Defence Council had the "power to formulate overall strategy and policy, enact rules and regulations and sit as the highest judicial body, the authority to implement and enforce its rulings rested largely with the individual leader-members or section and camp heads." [17]

---

16   A KLFA struggle-song records the event: When the war was declared in 1952, our country was turned into a huge prison. Innocent people, men, women and children were herded into concentration camps under all kinds of harsh repression. - Kinyatti (1980).
17 Bernett and Njama (1966). The following account on Kenya Defence Council and the Kenya
    Parliament are based on the this source.

The other important task of the Mwathe Conference was the election of the leadership of the Kenya Defence Council and also the organisation of all the fighting forces into eight armies. Kimathi was elected the President of the Kenya Defence Council, with Gen. Macharia Kimemia as vice-president, Gen. Kahiu-Itina as the Treasurer and Brig. Gathitu as Secretary.

Because of the particular needs of combining the military and political aspects of the anti-colonial armed struggle, there was a considerable overlap between the military and political leadership. Thus Kimathi was not only the President of the Kenya Defence Council; he was also the highest military authority as Field Marshal. The leadership was thus charged with the overall planning, organisation, and execution of both the aspects of the struggle, military and political.

The military force was divided into eight armies as follows:

1. Ituma Ndemi Army: Operating in the Nyeri District, commanded by Gen. Stanley Mathenge.

2. Gikuyu Iregi Army: Operating in the Murang'a District, commanded by Gen. Macaria Kimemia.

3. Kenya Inoro Army: Operating in the Kiambu District, commanded by Gen. Waruingi.

4. Mei Mathathi Army: Operating in the Mt. Kenya area, commanded by Gen. China.

5. Mburu Ngebo Army: Operating in the Rift Valley, commanded by Gen. Kimbo.

6. The Townwatch Battalions: Operating in all the urban areas. The fighters carried on normal civilian lives by day, but undertook active armed struggles at night or whenever necessary. Commanders varied from town to town and from time to time, in keeping with needs of warfare and security.

7. Gikuyu na Mumbi Trinity Army: Operated throughout the

country and consisted of all Mau Mau sympathisers, and also those who supported the struggle in different ways. It was this Army that helped with supplies and information on enemy activities. The actual participation of members varied.

8. Kenya Levellation Army: A complementary Army to the Townwatch Army, operating in the rural areas. The name implies the ideology of the freedom fighters, equality for all in society achieved through an armed struggle.

The Mwathe Conference was an important development. Not only did it put the armed forces on an organised war footing; it created a new united organisation which became the central policy making and administrative body with responsibilities covering the whole country, both over military and political matters. This was particularly important as the colonial regime had sought to kill the armed struggle by striking at the leadership and through them at the whole organisation without which the movement, they hoped, would just wither away.

By the formation of the Kenya Defence Council, Mau Mau created a new democratic political and military authority, which organised all the freedom fighters, their supporters and sympathisers. It was to the Kenya Defence Council that the struggling people looked as the new legal entity, which replaced the authority of the colonial administration. The Kenya Defence Council became the new beacon of hope for Kenyans under attack from a fierce, desperate enemy. It grew from the experiences of the previous years of struggle, suffering, imprisonment, torture, land and livestock confiscation and death. It also provided a foundation for the development of the future Kenya Parliament.

Soon after its formation, the Kenya Defence Council assessed the political situation and took action to support forces fighting colonialism. There had been a lot of adverse enemy propaganda condemning the freedom struggle as a backward movement. In order to give the correct picture and to achieve a greater unity among the freedom fighters and its supporters, it published a Charter, which set out its demands and aims. It was prepared by Kimathi under the authority of the Kenya Defence Council and came to be known as the Kimathi Charter. The Charter, reproduced below from Singh (1980), was widely circulated and it publicly and openly showed what Mau Mau and the people of Kenya were fighting for:

Kimathi Charter - We Reject Colonialism

We demand African self-government in Kenya.

We demand an African Magistrate's Court in full authority which will judge lawfully and righteously. We demand to know who hands over the money for land from Settlers and where the money goes.

We demand to know why many different Christian missions with different laws are brought to Kenya. Can one mission not suffice?

We demand authorities of gold, markets, roads, co-operative societies, and auctions to be in the hands of Africans.

We claim the full authority of making fire-arms and various kinds of weapons.

We demand that the European foreigners, rascals, troops and police should be withdrawn from Kenya African Reserves.

We reject imprisonment over Mau Mau.

We reject criminal or death cases to be judged by foreigners.

We condemn the dropping of poisons from the air as the colonialists in Kenya are doing to the African population.

We reject the foreign laws in Kenya, for they were not made for Kenya and are not righteous.

We reject being called terrorists when demanding our people's rights.

We demand a stop to the raping by foreigners of our wives and daughters; also female imprisonment and carrying of passes.

We reject foreign Attorney-General in Kenya, for he deals with appearance rather than righteousness. We reject the colonisation of Kenya, for in that state we are turned into slaves and beggars.

The publication of the Kimathi Charter by the Kenya Defence Council proved of immense importance in mobilising the people's forces to continue their anti-imperialist struggle. Thousands of workers and peasants had taken up arms against exploitation of their labour and stealing of their land and the Kimathi Charter articulated their demands. The Kenya Committee For Democratic Rights for Kenya Africans (1952-60) records the following from British press:

> The publication of the Kimathi Charter was timed to coincide with an important mass struggle being waged by the Kenya Land and Freedom Army. This was the bus boycott which was a protest against various aspects of imperialist control over the lives of people, and aimed at mobilising popular support to advance and promote the armed struggle. 23-9-53.

Singh (1980) sums up the importance of the Kimathi Charter and the bus boycott:

> The Charter gave great encouragement to the people of Kenya. It also gave impetus to the great demonstration of national unity and national struggle that was taking place at that time in Nairobi. This was the Bus Boycott which started on 23 September, 1953. Initiated by the Mau Mau freedom fighters, the Bus Boycott involved all the patriotic people. It was a national protest against the oppressive Emergency Regulations including: the introduction of History of Employment Cards (Green Cards); keeping African buses out of many locations in Nairobi; closer control over all Africans by forcing them into 'villages' (detention camps) surrounded by barbed wire with a police post in each 'village'; cancellation of (many) drivers' passes in the Rift Valley areas; restrictions on travelling; painting of names on bicycles; the order for yellow band 'marked' taxis.

> Above all, it was a protest against the imprisonment and detention of tens of thousands of patriots; against (Colonial) government's refusal to release the imprisoned and detained national leaders; and against the policies of the European Settlers' Organisation and the Electors Union, the main point of which was to "build a strong and prosperous state which will be a bulwark of the Commonwealth in British Africa maintaining British traditions of loyalty to the Crown." The Bus Boycott continued

for many months.

Thus by these various means, the Kenya Defence Council carried the struggle in the military field as well as at the popular mass-level to new heights. These led to many victories, which forced the colonialists to make token offers of reform, hoping thereby to divert the attention of the struggle. But the struggle continued.

The Kenya Parliament Takes Control - Kimathi is Prime Minister (1954)

As the armed conflict intensified, new contradictions, both antagonistic ones against the enemy, and non-antagonistic ones within Mau Mau, developed. Certain weaknesses of the Kenya Defence Council also emerged. It was found that in an attempt to make the Kenya Defence Council more democratic and representative, it had been made too large to be able to function efficiently in a war situation.

A meeting of the Kenya Defence Council was held in February 1954 in order to address these shortcomings. Eight hundred delegates attended the meeting and after intensive discussions, a decision was taken to replace the Kenya Defence Council by a new body - the Kenya Parliament. This was a change of fundamental importance. The Kenya Parliament was the first legitimate African Government of Kenya. Its aims were to separate political and military aspects of the struggle, making the former paramount, to emphasise the national character of the freedom movement, to ensure the representation of all Kenyan nationalities, and to assume authority over liberated and semi-liberated areas and people. Militarily, it established its authority over all fighting units and prepared a new military offensive. It also formulated a foreign policy and sent representatives to foreign governments.

Twelve members were elected to the Kenya Parliament, and Kimathi was elected the first Prime Minister. Their first loyalty was to the Kenya Parliament and not to their former armies. A new Field Marshal was elected. He was Macharia Kimemia. Kimathi was now free to devote full attention to the political sphere and to the affairs of Kenya Parliament. In addition, all the thirty-three districts of Kenya were represented in the Kenya Parliament, thus making it a national body.

One of the delegates at the meeting summed up the argument for the formation of the Kenya Parliament and saw its potential role, as recorded by Njama (Barnett and Njama, 1966):

> ...the thing we lack is a Kenya central (political) organisation which should be the Government. I think it is high time we elected our Kenya Parliament members and let them run the country ... the little we would have done (by this action) would be of great importance in Kenya's history, which will (record) that the Kenya Parliament was formed and maintained by warriors in Nyandarwa for so many years. As the Kenya Parliament shall govern Kenya, the founders' names shall live as long as the Kenya independent Government shall live.

The following were the first members of Kenya Parliament (in effect, the first Cabinet; other levels represented Kenyan districts):

Kimathi wa Waciuri - Prime Minister

Brig. Gen. Kahiu-Itina - Deputy Prime Minister

Gen. Kimbo Mutuku - Minister for Finances

Karari Njama - Chief Secretary

Gen. Ndiritu Thuita - Deputy Chief Secretary

Gen. Abdulla - Deputy Minister for Finance

Major Vindo*

Gen. Kirihinya*

Col. Kahii ka Arume*

Brig. Gathitu Waithaka*

Gen. Muraya Mbuthia*

Major Omera*

Gen. Rui*

* *varying responsibilities according to the needs at particular times.*

One major crisis that faced the Kenya Parliament was the capture of General China by the colonial forces and his subsequent betrayal to the enemy. The Kenya Parliament held a special session to discuss the crisis and to reply to the colonial government's offer to negotiate an end to hostilities. The reply is important for it sets out clearly the aims of the struggle and conditions for starting negotiations. The reply also demonstrated the strength of the armed forces. Among points made in the reply in February, 1954 (Barnett and Njama, 1966) were:

Land and Freedom Now

We are fighting for our lands - the Kenya Highlands which were stolen from the Africans by the Crown through the Orders in Council 1915, of the Crown Lands Ordinance which evicted Africans from their lands at present occupied by the Settlers or reserved for their future generations while landless Africans are starving of hunger or surviving on the same land as cheap labourers to the Settlers who were granted that land by the Crown.

Before we come out of the forest, the British Government must grant Kenya full independence under the African leadership, and also hand over all the alienated lands to Kenya African Government which will redistribute the land to its citizens.

If we do not get land and freedom now, we will continue to fight till the Government yields or the last drop of blood of our last fighter is spilt.

Now it is wartime; and war means destruction of everything without recognising children or their parents. War simply means taking away lives and wealth. The most civilised and advanced nations have failed to stop war as they believe that war is the only safeguard against slavery, oppression and exploitation by others.

It is now almost one and a half years since the declaration of the emergency. Every day since then you have been trying your best to destroy us completely, using nearly 100,000 strong force and dropping thousands of bombs on us from your jet fighters, Harvards and the heavy

Lincoln bombers. All your forces work day and night trying to finish us off, but you have not been successful, and you will not succeed. Though you think we are unarmed compared to your strength, we stand for right, we are confident of our victory. You may lose your empire in the course of impeding Kenya's independence.

The formation of the Kenya Parliament and the installation of Kimathi as the first Prime Minister of Kenya were events of great historical importance not only for Kenya, but for Africa as a whole and for the anti-colonial struggle generally.

Colonialism sought to suppress the dissemination of information about the formation of the free Government of Kenya under Kenya Parliament for fear that other colonies would also do the same. Yet the example of the Kenya Parliament remains forever as the greatest achievement of the Kenyan people in their anti-colonial warfare. The events of 1954 in Kenya were a herald of the events to come in other colonies: the final independence from colonialism as a result of fierce struggles. That this new historical era saw its first expression in Kenya was no small an achievement, given that colonialism had seen Kenya as a country of permanent European settlement and colonial control. The freedom fighters of Kenya showed, by their total commitment and sacrifice for the cause of national liberation, that no oppressed people can be exploited forever. Such was the magnitude of the achievement of Mau Mau forces. And Mau Mau's statement that "You may lose your empire in the course of impeding Kenya's independence" contained much truth, as events were to show.

Venys (1970) provides an overview of Mau Mau:

> The whole movement was organised in great detail and was very complex. It had two main wings which were usually called the "active wing" and the "passive wing". The former consisted of a number of fighting units forming together the Kenya Land Freedom Armies which finally concentrated in three main areas: the Aberdares, Mt. Kenya and Nairobi. The "passive wing" comprised various committees which were scattered all over the Kikuyu Land Unit as well as the capital. The movement had its headquarters in a central committee situated in Nairobi.

Mau Mau fighters and the people who worked with the armed forces sacrificed their property, the future of their families, faced colonial torture and suffered in colonial concentration camps and many perished under intense military attacks by the British forces. Their full history needs to be fully researched and made known to all.

Elements of Mau Mau Governance

The establishment of the Kenya Defence Council and particularly the Kenya Parliament with a Prime Minister and a cabinet were not mere trappings of power. They reflected Mau Mau's power over territories, people and institutions needed for exercising functions of a state. These included legal institutions, finance and taxation, communications, education, health and welfare of citizens, policing, security and military affairs, as reflected in the Cabinet of the Kenya Parliament. Mau Mau needed constitutional and policy frameworks to ensure it was capable of meeting needs of the people it controlled as well as the needs of waging a war - in the same way as the colonial government needed these. Its policies were reflected by, and were implemented through, its ideology, organisation, strategies and other related areas, which are examined below. These are the features that defined it as a civil administration as well as a fighting force. These two aspects - political and military - were clearly demarcated by the establishment of the Kenya Parliament. It is doubtful if the Mau Mau could have survived for years unless it had these essential elements of governance, which also looked forward to a post-independence Kenya. Alam and Gachihi (2007) reflect on the twin requirements of any revolutionary movement:

> For any revolutionary movement to succeed there must be plans [for] both organizational and military [aspects]. Mau Mau was no exception. It was a revolutionary movement against colonial oppression. The first phase of the movement involved establishing a network, contacts and a support base. Afterwards, the revolt was gradually transformed into a military campaign. These two phases are inseparable. Indeed, the success of the latter depends on the former.

Anti-Imperialist Ideology

The three strands of Mau Mau's ideological stand were anti-colonialism, anti-imperialism and a proletarian world outlook in the struggle against capitalism. They thus represented the unity of workers and peasants and all those who were not allied to the colonialists. This stand was derived from peasants' anti-colonial struggles, the trade union movement and working class struggles in the liberation struggle as well as from the nationalist forces resisting colonialism through political organisations over a long period.

Different aspects of the ideology became dominant at different times and freedom fighters responded differently at different times depending on the particular needs of each period. Just as at the political level different organisational structures were created in response to specific needs, so at the ideological level, different perspectives came to prominence in keeping with the specific contradictions and needs in the struggle at the specific times.

The ideological stand of the Kenya Defence Council and the Kenya Parliament were seen earlier. As time went on, there was a gradual shift in the struggle from an anti-colonial phase to an anti-neo-colonial one. This change in ideology reflected a change in the material condition at the time. In the period leading to independence and the period after independence, imperialism, the main force that Mau Mau fought, changed from colonialism to neo-colonialism. In keeping with this change, Mau Mau also changed its political and military priorities.

The class stand of Mau Mau was clear right from the beginning. The enemy was not seen in terms of the colour of their skin, as the colonialist propaganda had insisted, and in effect encouraged. Indeed, black Homeguard collaborators were prime target of revolutionary wrath. Kimathi explained in a letter he wrote from his headquarters in Nyandarwa in 1953, "the poor are the Mau Mau." Poverty can be stopped, he explained, "but not by bombs and weapons from the imperialists. Only the revolutionary justice of the struggles of the poor could end poverty for Kenyans" as Kimathi stated in his letter to the Nairobi newspaper, *Habari za Dunia.* (Odinga, 1968). Thus the movement was not against European people or Black people, but against colonialism and capitalism. It is also clear that Kimathi and the movement were taking a definite class stand.

Mau Mau was aware of the dangers that face a society when a rich minority sought privileges for itself at the expense of peasants and the workers. One high official in the Kenya Parliament warned of the dangers of such a situation, in a session in 1954 (Barnett and Njama, 1966):

> Some of us may seek privileges, but by the time we achieve our freedom you will have learnt to share a grain of maize or a bean amongst several people, feeling selfishness as an evil; and the hate of oppressing others would be so developed in you that you will not like to become another class of 'Black' European ready to oppress and exploit others just like the system we are fighting against.

Thus the battle was against oppression and exploitation. It is a reflection of the maturity of Mau Mau and of its deep understanding of imperialism and its grip on countries in the South that it was able to foresee the danger of imperialist control over newly independent countries in Africa even as it fought colonialism.

As the colonial phase was coming to an end, Mau Mau began to raise the concerns about its replacement by neo-colonialism. This brought the ideological battle to the forefront. It became necessary to place before the people a correct analysis of historical events, and to emphasise the need to continue the struggle. This was done in the form of a Policy Document, which was widely circulated. It was also presented at the Conference of the Kenya African National Union held in Nairobi in December 1961, where contradictions were developing about the need to combat neo-colonialism. The Document, entitled *The Struggle For Kenya's Future (1972)* was the clearest statement on the dangers of neo-colonialism. It is reproduced in Appendix B with a note by one of the writers. A brief selected section below provides clarity about what the ideological stand of activists in the War of Independence was:

> The struggle for Kenya's future is being waged today on three distinct though interrelated levels - political, racial and economic. It seems to us that we Africans are being allowed to "win" in the first two spheres as long as we don't contest the battle being waged on the third, all-important economic level.

It is this ideological stand of the War of Independence and of Mau Mau that the departing colonialists and the arriving neo-colonialists have sought to shut out from history books and from people's consciousness. It is the "properly indoctrinated group of the 'right kind' of Africans" who are today overseeing the process of averting a "*genuine* social revolution" but which still remains the goal of those struggling for liberation to this day.

Barnett and Njama (1966) sum up the importance of organisation and ideology in a revolution - the two aspects of Mau Mau's work:

> Just as any revolution requires a certain minimum amount of organization, a people in revolt requires an ideology. Without a set of ideas and ideals, few people are willing to risk their lives in revolutionary action. In Kenya, it is unlikely that the revolution would have occurred but for the integrative ideology developed over a period of thirty-odd years by numerous political, educational and trade union associations which articulated and brought in focus various grievances and set forward certain political, economic and social objectives.

Furedi (1989) looks at the links between a strong ideology and a strong organisation that Mau Mau demonstrated:

> Interpretations which portray Mau Mau as a centrally organized institution find their strongest support on the level of ideology. All sections of the movement articulated a similar ideology. Public pronouncements and petitions used similar language and put forward shared objectives whether from Nairobi, Nyeri or Elburgon.

It is this ideological stand and the organisational strength of Mau Mau that neo-colonialism and the comprador regime find difficult to accept.

Organisation

No struggle as large and facing a vastly superior military power as did Mau Mau could have existed without a strong organisation. The organisational strength of the movement needs to be recognised. Edgerton (1990) provides a succulent summary of Mau Mau's organisational structure:

> The Mau Mau movement was directed by what they usually called

"Muhimu," or the Central Committee. The Central Committee consisted of 12 men, including Kubai and Kaggia, with Eliud Mutonyi as its chairman. When the police began to make arrests at oathing ceremonies, the Central Committee created another group, known as the "30 Committee," to direct oathing and to shield the true directorate from government detection. Under the direction of Fred Kubai, the 30 men on this committee were responsible for coordinating the activities of local leaders in the tribal reserves and townships. In addition, the leaders of Mau Mau were advised by what they called the KAU Study Circle, a kind of brain trust composed of four or five KAU members and an equal number of outsiders who were sympathetic to KAU's stated goals. These men prepared background research on policy matters that the Central Committee might need to address in Kenya, as well as international concerns, especially ways of attracting foreign support.

At the same time, Edgerton (1990) provides records that show that Mau Mau was more interested in their political principles and in working class interests rather than racial background in their organisation or outlook:

Curious as it may seem in retrospect, the leaders of Mau Mau allowed three non Africans to serve on the Study Circle. One, Pio de Gama Pinto, was a Goan. Two were Europeans: Peter Wright, a former professor of history at Cawnpore, India, who served as a Lieutenant-Colonel in the British Intelligence Corps during World War II, and John P. B. Miller, a former Royal Navy Lieutenant Commander, then a resident of Kenya. The Study Circle originally met in the Nairobi offices of the Indian National Congress, and later, as police surveillance tightened, in private homes.

The formation of the Kenya Defence Council and of the Kenya Parliament indicates the importance that Mau Mau gave to organisations at national level. Its organisational structures at other levels have also been well documented, for example by Barnett and Njama (1966) and Mathu (1974).

Further evidence of Mau Mau's strong organizational structure is provided by Edgerton (1990):

[No rebels fought from forest camps. The rebellion also depended on the support of sympathizers in the reserves, and in Nairobi and other towns. Until mid-1954, the Central Committee and its War Council still purchased weapons, organized food supplies, and recruited new fighters for the forest armies. These new recruits were issued special identification cards in order to prevent infiltration by government informers. Meanwhile, men and women in the Kikuyu, Embu, and Meru reserves continued to supply money, information, food, and weapons. Many risked their lives as often as those who fought in the forest. In fact, much of the actual fighting was done by men and women who lived in the reserves, and in Nairobi or smaller towns. Units from the forests often entered the reserves at night, and spent the day sleeping in the houses of sympathizers or hiding in a secluded area, before carrying out their raids and returning to camp. But others who had never entered the forests were sometimes called into action by a local leader, usually with the approval of higher Mau Mau authority. Sometimes they were ordered to kill a Kikuyu traitor, at other times to raid a Homeguard or police post for weapons]. *sic*

This is a far cry from the picture of Mau Mau painted by "local white Settlers who painted it as dark and satanic in content and inspiration" (Maloba, 1998).

Strategy

The strategy that Mau Mau used against a militarily stronger enemy was crucial in its struggle. Mau Mau saw Kenyan peoples' contradiction with imperialism as an antagonistic one, which could not be resolved peacefully. It thus used the method of armed struggle, guerrilla warfare and people's struggle against imperialism. But it made a distinction between the three aspects of the enemy. Against the colonial military forces, it used the method of guerrilla warfare and military battles (both offensive and defensive), which included attacks on military targets, on prisons to free captured guerrilla fighters, and on armouries to procure arms.

The other 'face' of the enemy was white Settlers, many of whom benefited from free or cheap land and who had taken up arms against the people of Kenya. The Mau Mau movement used another method to deal with this threat. The Settlers' main concern was to protect 'their' property on which their wealth depended. Indeed, their main aim in settling in Kenya was to appropriate, or acquire very cheaply, peasant land and labour and use it to produce wealth for themselves. The freedom fighters attacked them where it hurt most: the property itself. This served not only to threaten the very economic base of the Settlers; it also helped the guerrillas to procure food and rations they needed to continue their armed struggle, thus providing the material base for the armed revolution.

Mau Mau used yet another method against the third face of the enemy, the African Homeguards. Considering that many had been forced either by economic reasons or through force or ignorance to become collaborators, many of those considered capable of reforming were given advance warnings to stop betraying the cause of national liberation. Only when these were ignored was action taken against them, depending on the seriousness of their collaboration, but sanctioned by Mau Mau courts. In this way many who had initially sided with the enemy were won over to the nationalist side and some of them then made important contribution to the anti-imperialist struggle. Many whose economic base was tied too strongly to imperialism refused to reform and had to be dealt with more severely so that they did not pose a threat to the armed resistance forces.

Another tactic used against the collaborators involved information warfare or propaganda aimed at demoralising them. An example of this was spreading favourable news about guerrilla successes in enemy held territory. Pinning large notices on trees and walls near schools, police stations and social halls was one such way. It was not only the message of these posters that put fear in the enemy but the very fact that such notices could be placed in areas under colonial control. Despite the fact that strict security measures were taken by the colonial armed forces, the Mau Mau activists managed to reach areas in the very heart of the city to pin these posters thus showing their strength and demoralising enemy soldiers and civilians.

It would be wrong to deny that there were contradictions among the ranks of Mau Mau fighters and among the people. These became sharper under enemy attack. But these were not antagonistic ones, at least at the beginning, and were resolved by the use of non-violent means. In the main, democratic methods were used to resolve these contradictions. One of the aims of Mau Mau was to form a democratic society where everyone would have equal rights and duties and a equal access to the wealth produced by their joint labour. They put their ideas into practice in the liberated areas even as they engaged the enemy in a fierce battle.

The democratic method involved the use of meetings, conferences, and congresses where free discussions could be held and ideas could be expressed without fear of persecution. After long discussions, decisions would be taken on basis of majority vote. Questions of leadership were settled through secret ballots and elections were held at every level in so far as war conditions allowed. An example of such a conference was the Mwathe Conference mentioned earlier. Elections were held, for example, when Kimathi was elected the Prime Minister. These democratic discussions and elections helped to formulate new policies and to resolve many contradictions. In addition, free exchange of ideas was encouraged to allow the people a chance to hear views of their leaders and to give their views to the leadership.

Mau Mau's military strategy ensured that the military might of the greatest military power at the time was kept at bay for over four years. Kaggia, B, Leeuw and Kaggia, M (2012) sum up their achievements:

> In the battle Mau Mau soldiers distinguished themselves as great guerrilla fighters. General Sir George Erskine, a British general advised his Government that Mau Mau could not be stamped out by force. Although the general was soon to be removed from command, what he said was true and the Government eventually had to accept it in practice. The British couldn't crush Mau Mau with all their sophisticated weapons. Considering the difficult conditions under which the Mau Mau soldiers fought and lived, it is impossible to ignore their greatness. They managed to fight the war for more than four years.

> Mau Mau's political and military strategy were well aligned to its overall vision of creating a nation free from foreign domination and with policies meeting the needs of its people, not corporations and Settlers.

Utavumilia Kifo? - A Mau Mau song 18

Watoto wa Kenya huishi mwituni
Wakinyeshewa na mvua
Wakipata njaa,
Mateso na baridi nyingi
Kwa upendo wa udongo.

Uui, iiyai, uui, iiyai
Kuuawa na taabu na kufungwa
Mara nyingi
Je, utavumilia?

Na akina nani hao wanaimba kwa sauti kubwa
Ngambo ya pili ya mto
Wakiwaimbia Kago na Mbaria
Watafutaji wa haki.

English translation:

'Are You Ready to Face Death?'

Kenya's children live in forests
They are soaked in heavy rains
They go hungry, endure hardships
They live through cold days and nights
All because of the love of their country

Woe! Woe! Woe! Woe!
Are you ready to endure all these hardships?
Are you ready to face prisons and detention camps?
Tell me, are you ready to face death?

Whose are those voices raised in song

---

18   This Mau Mau song was released by the Tamaduni Players of Nairobi during their production of
      Mzalendo Kimathi, a play on the Kenyan struggle written by Ngugi wa Thiong'o and Micere Githae
      Mugo (1978). The Tamaduni Production performed at the University of Nairobi in early 1980s.

From across the river
Singing praises of Kago and Mbaria
Champions of truth, fighters for democratic right
Whose are those voices?

Infrastructure

There is no doubt that Mau Mau was well organised as a military and as a political organisation. The colonialists were aware of their abilities, as they had discovered many examples of infrastructure in towns and forests even as the War of Independence was going on. They deliberately chose to hide these facts and set out to destroy such evidence so as to continue their myth that Mau Mau was a primitive group of people who had nothing to do with the War of Liberation. Such structures included hospitals, libraries, social halls as well as rules and regulations and records of civil and legal practice that guided the movement. Additional ones, given below, are taken from the Press Briefings compiled by Kenya Committee For Democratic Rights for Kenya Africans (1952-60):

- During Operation Epsom... a large encampment furnished as a high court, and also a well built installation like a barracks, with numbered rooms and a well-equipped kitchen with accommodation for 60 people was discovered. (19-6-53).

- An army patrol following in the tracks of freedom fighters discovered a 40 bed hospital with complete medical kits. A Government communiqué said the hospital was 5 miles east of Mount Kinangop. 13-7-54.

- A Rifle Brigade tracker team in the N.E. Aberdare discovered a thatched building with a notice "Government House" written on it, and found 25 binoculars, a structure resembling a church, with seating for 90 people, and a hide-out. 27-5-55.

- Security Forces searching the Aberdare Forest found a deserted hospital which had apparently been evacuated a few days before, found also was a Council Chamber with accommodation for about 150. 6-6-55.

Newspaper and other reports built up a fuller picture, as quoted earlier in this book:

- Reports so far received (as part of Operation Hammer) (reveal) the significant feature of the first phase has been the large number of hideouts found (in the Aberdare forests), some considerable in size and many were skilfully constructed. One consisted of four huts capable of holding 80 men and with a piped water supply from a waterfall 30 yards away. [19] [p70]

- On the outskirts of Nairobi, Kikuyu guards and men of the Kenya Regiment killed four freedom fighters, destroyed a Mau Mau hospital furnished with a supply of medicine and food, and arrested six women food carriers.[20] [p.70]

A number of reports on Mau Mau gun factories, conference facilities, as well as housing and water supply systems in liberated areas were carried in newspaper reports:

· East African Command headquarters announced today that a patrol of guards and police from the Meru (nationality) led by Officer Harry Hinde discovered and destroyed a Mau Mau arms factory in the Meru forest. [21]

· Police today discovered a Mau Mau gun shop and store in a part of Nairobi where the city's two hundred street sweepers live. [22]

· In early days the terrorist camps were well built. The sites were laid out with solidly constructed huts of split bamboo, with kitchens and stores, quarters for women and children and signboards indicating the commander of the camp ... from these camps, arms and ammunition, food, clothing and valuable documents have been recovered. [23]

The Kenya Committee Press Extracts summarises reports from contemporary

---

19 Times (London), 14 January, 1955.
20 Kenya Committee. Press Extracts, Vol.1 (25 September, 1954), pp. 82-83.
21 Manchester Guardian. 29 Jan.1954.
22 Manchester Guardian. 23 Feb. 1954.
23 East African Standard. 20 August, 1954.

papers about the destruction of Mau Mau hospitals by the British forces:

> An army patrol following in the tracks of freedom fighters discovered a
> 40 bed Mau Mau hospital with complete medical kits. A Government
> communiqué said the hospital was 5 miles east of Mount Kinangop.[24]

*

> Security Forces searching the Aberdare Forests found a deserted hospital
> which had apparently been evacuated a few days before, found also was
> a Council Chamber with accommodation for about 150.[25]

There are various accounts of Mau Mau gun factories and some of these are
still available. Kinyatti (2008) says: "The Shauri Moyo and Pumwani bases
played a special role as KLFA gun factories. Karura Forest was the main
KFLA gun factory in Nairobi. It was also a KLFA major hospital." There
were many South Asian skilled craftsmen who helped the establishment of such
factories and training Mau Mau cadres in gun making. One such person was
Jaswant Singh who was sentenced to death for illegally possessing two rounds
of ammunition. As the London *Times* noted: "...this was the first time that
the supreme penalty has been imposed on a non-African under the emergency
regulations."[26] (Kinyatti, 2008) provides some details:

> Jaswant Singh was storing firearms for the Movement. His house was
> a safe haven for the Movement. In 1954, he was betrayed, arrested and
> sentenced to death for possession of firearm. Despite the savage torture
> he underwent he refused to betray the Movement.

> Durrani, Nazmi (2017). provides further information on him:

> Jaswant Singh lived in Molo. By profession he was a carpenter, mason,
> plumber, electrician, builder, radio and motor mechanic, welder, lorry
> driver, tractor driver and gun maker (a karigar). He secretly supplied
> material to manufacture weapons, guns and ammunition, to Mau Mau
> fighters active in the Rift Valley area.

---

24   Kenya Committee. Press Extracts, Vol.1 (13 July, 1954), p.67.
25   Kenya Committee. Press Extracts, Vol. 1 (6 June, 1955), p.140.
26   Times (London). 31 July, 1954.

Other reports of Mau Mau gun factories, conference facilities, as well as housing and water supply systems in liberated areas were carried in newspaper reports:

- East African Command headquarters announced today that a patrol of guards and police from the Meru (nationality) led by Officer Harry Hinde discovered and destroyed a Mau Mau arms factory in the Meru forest.[27]

- Police today discovered a Mau Mau gun shop and store in a part of Nairobi where the city's two hundred street sweepers live.[28]

- In early days the terrorist camps were well built. The sites were laid out with solidly constructed huts of split bamboo, with kitchens and stores, quarters for women and children and signboards indicating the commander of the camp ... from these camps, arms and ammunition, food, clothing and valuable documents have been recovered.[29]

These are but a few examples of Mau Mau infrastructures. Others can be seen in the narratives of many books written by Mau Mau activists as well as in official colonial records. Here is an important area for research, particularly among surviving Mau Mau activists, to provide a fuller picture of this important aspect of Mau Mau organisation.

Politics of Information [30]

Mau Mau's information and communication strategy reflects different aspects of its overall work. Each of the elements of governance mentioned above, such as ideology, organisation and strategy, required effective flow of information between different units and parts of the resistance movement. This flow was the lifeblood of the organisation. This is essential in peacetime in any organisation, but was of particular significance in an underground movement facing a war situation against a heavily armed enemy. Survival depended on this life-giving process of flow of information and communication. And yet this was difficult to

---

27   Manchester Guardian. 29 Jan.1954.
28   Manchester Guardian. 23 Feb. 1954.
29   East African Standard. 20 August, 1954.
30   This section includes material from Durrani, Shiraz (2006).

achieve in the war situation created by the imposition of the State of Emergency by British colonialism which relied not only on its military and political might but also on its experience of oppression in its other colonies, particularly India and Malaysia. The difficulties for Mau Mau were compounded by information embargoes by colonialism and the absence of global networks such as the Internet. Thus experiences from the resistance forces in India and other countries were not easily available to the resistance organisation. It was to prevent the availability of such information that the Kenya colonial government banned various progressive publications, including many from USSR, Peoples Republic of China and India, as mentioned in Durrani, S. (2006).

That Mau Mau managed to develop a sophisticated information policy and practice is a reflection of its strength as an advanced 20th Century resistance movement. This is again another area that requires much research. This section attempts a brief overview of its information and communication strategy.

Communications

Mau Mau realised that any serious confrontation with a technically superior power required good organisation and planning. A key requirement to meet this was the establishment of an efficient and effective communications strategy. The information and communications structures had to be strong. These had to be created in secret and on a national scale. The task was made more difficult as the enemy they faced had the resources of its whole colonial empire. As the number of people involved in the anti-colonial struggle was very large and spread out over a vast area, the problems of communications had to be solved first. An organisation of this vast magnitude could not function unless its various components could communicate with each other: the leadership needed to get intelligence and other reports from the smallest units and pass down instructions for action. At the same time contacts with sympathetic masses of workers and peasants as well as links with nationalities from all parts of the country had to be maintained.

Different methods of communication were developed and used at different stages of the struggle and in different areas of the country, depending on the intensity of struggle in each area and on whether the area was liberated, semi-liberated or under British control. Mau Mau developed an information strategy, which included the following aspects:

1. Oral communications.
2. Revolutionary publishing.
3. Use of pamphlets and handbills.
4. Establishment of a people's press.
5. Information gathering and dissemination.[31]

At the time of the Declaration of Emergency, there was need to organise secretly. The colonial regime had kept Kenyan nationalities in isolation from each other by banning Kenya-wide nationalist movements. This had been overcome at one level by various nationality-based organisations working closely together. But one of the first tasks for Mau Mau was to develop new communication links with all people of Kenya, and to do it secretly.

Mau Mau, using its organisational network which was based at Mathare Valley, a working class residential area in Nairobi, solved this problem. Since the largest concentration of workers was in Nairobi, communications and organisational networks reaching all parts of the country were organised from here. Workers of various nationalities were recruited from here. There were close links between the militant trade unions and the central command of Mau Mau. The politically aware and class-conscious workers recruited in Nairobi acted not only as cadres in the city but they helped to set up powerful links with the peasants. Workers of different nationalities became in effect links between peasants, plantation and urban workers and Mau Mau. Particularly important was the information collected by workers in domestic service, offices, and plantations. Workers in government departments were particularly important as they collected information from conversations, official files, newspapers and other reports and passed it on to Mau Mau using oral means of communication. It was this flow of information that enabled Mau Mau to be more effective in all its work. Without such links the resistance movement could easily have been crushed by imperialism in a short time. Historical studies that see Mau Mau as a peasant movement only miss this important aspect of working class input into the War

31 Further details on Mau Mau's communications policy and practice are covered in Durrani, Shiraz (2006).

of Independence.

The process of communications was made easy by using the central position of Nairobi as the transport hub of Kenya. The railways provided links from Mombasa to Kisumu and messages could be passed on by workers on the railways all along the route of the railway. Within urban areas, taxi drivers provided well-developed means of communications. In addition, Mau Mau developed bicycle networks to supplement other means of communicating and connecting its various support structures. Such an approach developed on the practices developed by the trade unions which had used such methods to gain strength during their strike and other activities and for recruiting members, as described by Makhan Singh (1969).

Kenya's experience in using transport facilities and workers involved in running them - taxi drivers, buses, trains etc - has a parallel with the experience in Cuba, as recalled by Quinn (2015):

> Taken together, the workers' struggles provide a compelling account of how organized labour contributed directly and indirectly to help shape the course of revolutionary struggle in 1950s Cuba. As Cushion [2016] depicts so vividly here, workers provided valuable material support for the rebel guerrillas in a number of ways, including organizing significant strike action in support of the Granma landing and armed uprising in Santiago. Workers in shops, warehouses, and distribution depots proved valuable through large-scale pilfering of essentials; railway workers were able to move those supplies under the noses of the police; bus drivers formed propaganda distribution networks, while telephone operators eavesdropped on police conversations, providing vital intelligence for those more directly engaged in the armed struggle. Others organized clandestine networks involved in acts of sabotage such as derailing an armoured train carrying soldiers sent to protect the vital railway system, and helping disaffected soldiers to desert. Such actions depended on a high degree of organization that reached its apotheosis in the revolutionary general strike of January 1, 1959. Overlooked in much of the literature, this strike is reassessed here for its decisive contribution to the triumph of the revolution … Thus, for Cushion, the final victory of the revolutionary forces should be viewed as the result of a combination

of armed guerrilla action and mass support.

Of course the situation of working the class and the level of class struggles in Kenya were quite different from those in Cuba. Yet it is true that in Kenya, as in Cuba, resistance forces worked as a partnership between armed guerrilla units and mass support. Lessons in analysing Kenyan history can be learnt from the Cuban experience. Similarly, understanding the role of peasants in the revolutions in Vietnam, China and Cuba can find parallels in the experience in Kenya. The struggle against colonialism and imperialism is universal in many countries but the particular manifestations of these struggles vary from country to country. Within these boundaries, understanding the forces of resistance and oppression can help in learning lessons not only in how to conduct anti-imperialist struggles, but also how to understand and communicate information and history from a working class perspective.

After the Declaration of Emergency by the Colonial authorities, it became necessary for Mau Mau activists to go underground but the movement functioned very efficiently as an organisation. This is shown, for example, in its communication activities. The colonial administration took over total control of all the mass media upon Declaration of Emergency. Until then, Mau Mau had been publishing over fifty newspapers in Kiswahili and in various nationality languages, as well as a large number of struggle songs and other anti-colonial material. The Emergency measures were now used to suppress all these publications, which had functioned as important means of communication with the supporters of Mau Mau.

Mau Mau soon found alternative methods of communicating not only with the active fighters, but also with the masses who supported it and whose armed fist it was. Oral media were extensively used. Established printing presses, particularly those owned by progressive South Asian Kenyans were used. Cyclostyling machines were installed at their Mathare Valley Headquarters. All these were used to issue hand bills, posters and newspapers. Mau Mau published the *High Command* which was issued regularly between 1952 and 1957. Asian Kenyan cadres and supporters of Mau Mau initially printed this, as they could initially escape colonial suspicion. Later, it was printed at its Mathare Valley printing works. *High Command* was anti-imperialist in content and circulated underground among the 35,000 freedom fighters and provided a basic forum for the politicisation and advancement of the combatants. It informed them on the ideology, the organisation, the strategies, and activities of the Revolution. (Mirii, 1979).

One task facing Mau Mau was that of ensuring the political and ideological development of its cadres. The other was to demoralise the enemy troops and their White settler supporters. Many handbills and posters were issued and posted at prominent places in enemy areas. One pamphlet was issued just three days after the Declaration of Emergency. It was sent to many Settlers and posted on trees and walls in many areas of Nairobi. This shows the organisation commanded by the resistance forces. While the colonial armies were busy creating a reign of terror, cadres were printing and distributing important communications under enemy gunfire. One such pamphlet is important also for its content, which shows the clear understanding of the situation by Mau Mau. It was addressed to the "Murdering Colonialists" and was entitled *Fascism Has Come to Kenya*. It read:

Fascism Has Come to Kenya

You must feel very happy at the outward success of your cruel operation. You arrested our leaders and a lot of other people. Thousands of Africans leading a normal life have been stopped, searched, beaten, humiliated and arrested. Creating the Emergency, you have brutally treated us and now you cannot claim democracy and freedom. Fascism has come to Kenya.

We have been robbed of all freedom. You have destroyed our press by arresting our editors and suppressing our newspapers. But you cannot suppress the voice of the people. The brutality and oppression, the show of force and the rule of gun will not stop us from our goal. You cannot end our political wish by arresting our leaders. We have many more men with brains and will continue to fight you and achieve our freedom. This is the voice of new Africa. We have been forced to go underground. If we are known, you will murder us. We are not afraid. We ask how many of us you will imprison, how many of us you will kill? We are six million and power is in our numbers. We shall retaliate in the method you have employed. We shall not forget the bad treatment we are suffering. When our time comes we shall not show mercy, because you do not know what mercy is. We will kill you like you are murdering us today. This is no threat. It is how we are feeling today. Africans unite! [32]

Oral Communications

The use of oral communication systems was well established before the colonial government declared a state of Emergency. Fred Kubai (1983) explains how this developed:

> In November 1951 the colonialists and white settler newspapers stopped covering KAU public meetings. [In order to overcome] this, the militants started mouth-to-mouth bush-radio information service. Songs were composed carrying revolutionary and 'subversive' messages and were sung by both young and old. Kinuthia Mugia of Olenguroine became champion in the composition of new Kikuyu songs. J. J. Gakara, among others, printed the songs into 'hymn books'. Kikuyu and Kiswahili newspapers and pamphlets were started. I revived the official KAU organ, *Sauti-Ya-Mwafrika*. Other militant papers included *Afrika Mpya* which was edited by Kaggia, *Hindi ya Gikuyu* and *Muthamaki*, which were edited by Victor Wokabi, *Muramati, Mumenyereri*; *Kayu-ka-Embu, Wihuge, Gikuyu na Mumbi*.

The content of these publications reflect a high awareness of what imperialism meant for Kenya. For example, Kinyatti (2008) quotes from *Muthamaki* which explained the conditions which gave rise to Mau Mau in an article in July 1952:

> Mau Mau will never be destroyed by the imposition of fines, imprisonment or torture. Mau Mau is the product of the exploitation and racism which our people experience in their daily lives. Eliminate exploitation and racism and there will be no Mau Mau.

There was a need to organise secretly against colonialism. This was achieved by

---

32 A copy of the pamphlet was sent to the 'Kenya Committee for Democratic Rights for Kenya' in London, from whose files it is quoted here. The Committee was formed in solidarity with the people of Kenya in their struggle against imperialism. So alarmed were the Colonial Government authorities by the content of this pamphlet that the Colonial Attorney General, Mr. John Whyatt, prevented any newspaper from printing it 'on threat of prosecution'.

using oral communication, a method developed during an earlier period when the colonialist regime had banned Kenya-wide nationalist movements, in order to keep Kenyan nationalities in isolation from each other.

The problem of how to communicate effectively, but secretly, was solved by Mau Mau using its organisational network, centred at Mathare Valley in Nairobi. Since the largest concentration of workers was in Nairobi, a new communication network was organised from here. Workers of various nationalities were recruited in Nairobi. One aspect of their work was to act as links with their nationality areas. Thus the worker-organised Mau Mau movement established deep roots among peasantry, without which the whole movement could have been crushed by imperialism within a short time.

This early organisational work, together with the task of establishment of communication links with the rest of the country, was done so secretly that it was almost five years before the colonial government became aware of the movement and were forced to declare a State of Emergency - in effect a state of war - against Kenyan workers and peasants in October, 1952.

Before the Emergency was declared, the nationalist and the worker forces had been using the "legal" press to organise and communicate, although this had to be done in coded languages which outsiders could not understand. One aspect of the political work was to organise mass political meetings, which could both organise people and give direction to the political movement. It was thus necessary to communicate times and places of such anti-imperialist meetings to the people who were ever eager to be active. Barton (1979) examines this early period to assess how the communication needs were satisfied:

> The mushrooming of the African press was an important factor in fostering political action in the urban centres of Kenya after the Second World War. Publications appeared in several (national) languages and also in English. Most of these were printed in Nairobi, although Mombassa had the *Coast African Express* and on the shores of Lake Victoria, in Kisumu, there was the *Nyanza Times*.

> All were nationalist and highly militant, expressing bitterness at colonial discrimination and poverty and insecurity of the African [people] against the affluence of the Settlers.

The Kikuyu papers around Nairobi were the most successful, and the most influential was *Mumenyereri* ("Defender"). This was a weekly edited by the Kenya African Union's assistant general secretary, Henry Mworia, and with a sale of 10,000 was probably read by six times that number.

As the tension grew which was to ignite finally in the Mau Mau, it became more and more uncompromising in its nationalism. The colonial government had banned political meetings but *Mumenyereri* was regularly referring to 'tea parties' in the shanty towns (Mathare, Kariobangi, Bahati and Majengo worker areas) around Nairobi, which were, in fact, occasions for the secret [anti-imperialist] oathing ceremonies.

Kinyatti (2008) gives an even higher estimate of the circulation of *Mumenyereri*:

As channels of political communications, and using our own languages, these anti-imperialist newspapers were vital in developing anti-imperialist consciousness amongst the Kenyan masses. Some of them were widely read and had great political influence in the country. For instance, *Mumenyereri* was the most popular paper in Central Kenya and the squatter areas of the Rift Valley, with an average circulation of 20,000 copies. It played a patriotic role in agitating against British colonial land and labour policy, vehemently opposed white racism and cultural imperialism, and supported the underground movement.

After the Declaration of Emergency by the Colonial authorities, it became necessary for the Mau Mau to reorganise as an underground movement. But it continued to function very efficiently as an organisation. This is shown, for example, in its communication activities. The colonial administration took total control over all the mass media upon Declaration of Emergency. Until then, the Mau Mau had been publishing directly or indirectly over fifty newspapers in Kiswahili and in various nationality languages, and had published a large number of liberation songs and other anti-colonial material. The Emergency measures were now used by the colonial power to suppress all these publications, which had functioned as important means of communication for the liberation forces.

When the British colonial administration became aware of the full extent of the organisation with its specific ideology and strategies for liberation backed by a political and military power, it began to investigate the background and organisation of the movement. Leakey (1954) had this to say about Mau Mau's intelligence gathering, and its development and use of the oral medium:

> The value of good intelligence system has always been appreciated by the Kenyan people. The Mau Mau organised a system of getting their own followers into key positions where they could find out what was happening and report to their leaders. Chosen men obtained positions as houseboys and chauffeurs in the household where there was the greatest likelihood of being able to learn things about the plans of Security Forces. Others were encouraged to get jobs in Government Offices, in the Police, and in the Homeguards and Telephone Service. Since the Kikuyu have always supplied a very high proportion of the employees of these categories in normal times and since there are generally loyal Kikuyu in such jobs, it was and still is very difficult indeed to distinguish between the spy and the genuine loyalist.
>
> Moreover, by no means all those employed on such intelligence work were drawn from the ranks of the Kikuyu. Enough members of other tribes had been won over to the Mau Mau cause to make it possible to use members of these other tribes in this intelligence organisation.

It is interesting to note that when the colonial authorities wanted to minimise the national significance of Mau Mau, their propaganda described Mau Mau as a; purely Gikuyu movement; yet, as the above clearly indicates, the national spread of the movement is freely acknowledged by colonial sources.

Oral communication was considered a safe means of communication by the liberation forces because of the high security risks in written communications. It was common for a team of two or more Mau Mau activists to carry messages from the Mau Mau High Command in the heart of Nyandarua to different Mau Mau centres, and its armies, or to the progressive workers and peasants throughout the country. The art of the progressive Wakamba wood carvers (*carving* no. 1) depicts the scene:

Two couriers carrying orders from the Kenya Defence Council are caught in the enemy ambush. One courier rushes at the enemy so that the other may escape and deliver the orders. The dying fighter digs deep the soil and exhorts his companion to continue. The courier crosses many ridges and valleys across Kenya. (*History of Kenya*, 1976).

These activists performed many tasks: soldiers, librarians (with duties ranging from collection, storage and making available the intelligence from different units), social workers and hunters (to obtain food while on missions). The soldier-information workers avoided carrying any written material on their bodies. They had developed their memories and could carry detailed instructions in their heads. They were under specific instructions that should they meet the enemy, they were not to risk their lives but ensure that their messages were delivered. Many brave soldier-information workers gave their lives during the struggle while ensuring that communications lines were kept open.

The Mau Mau movement had developed a large number of such soldier-information workers who knew the land routes for safe travel. At the same time they had developed a network of small libraries and archival units in the liberated areas which contained much useful information. The colonial authorities found details of advanced Mau Mau practices in the course of one of their mass arrest campaigns, as quoted by the *Times* (London, 11-08-1954):

> Arrests made in operation "Broom"...The search revealed that the Mau Mau had begun to use as couriers persons not likely to be suspected, among them a large number of young boys and old men. One deformed elderly man who was identified as a collector of funds had £40 hidden among beggars' rags when arrested.

Again, the *Times* (London, 30-09-1954) reports:

> Brigadier Boyce, general secretary of the Save the Children Fund, said that in the reserves there are children whose fathers have been killed, others whose families had left their homes, and many more whose fathers had gone away. In Nairobi, it was estimated that there were up to 1,000 such children. "Many of the orphans and homeless boys are acting as food carriers and couriers to the Mau Mau gangs, and eventually become

recruits to Mau Mau," he added.

Oral communication was used in other areas as well. It was particularly useful in working with the masses, for example, in passing messages about meetings or plans about specific military engagement. It was in this way that active and progressive workers and peasants passed on news about enemy movements to the military command. Children and women played a central part in this as, initially at least, they were not suspected to be Mau Mau activists. The use of resistance songs continued in detention camps. The *Kenya Committee Press Extracts* (Vol. 1, 07-05-1954) records:

> Most of the women showed quite openly their support for the freedom fighters while detained in screening camps. At one camp the women danced and sang Mau Mau songs. When some of them were escorted to the trains they hurled their rations of tinned meat, milk and biscuits at the railway staff.

The colonial administration was so concerned about singing of Mau Mau songs that it sentenced people to solitary confinement for this "crime", as the following report in the *Manchester Guardian* (30-05-1956) shows:

> ...Cases which Miss Eileen Fletcher (a former rehabilitation officer in Kenya) described yesterday included one in which Kikuyu women were given sixteen days' solitary confinement in small dark cells made of corrugated iron, for singing Mau Mau hymns.

Another aspect of Mau Mau's guerrilla and communications strategy was to feed incorrect information to the colonial forces. They also deprived the colonial forces of information altogether, so that often the colonial forces acted in total ignorance about Mau Mau movements, force strength and plans. This obviously could not have been achieved without the support of the masses in towns as well as in the countryside. This was acknowledged in the Kenya Police Annual Report for 1954:

> The year opened with the initiative in the hands of Mau Mau which... had virtually put a stop to the flow of information to the authorities. The vast majority of the Kikuyu (people) was either, actively or passively, assisting the Mau Mau movement.

This was confirmed by the British Parliamentary delegation, which visited Kenya. Its report, published on 23 February 1955 and quoted in the *Times* (24-02-1955), contrasts the use of information as a weapon by the two opposing forces:

> The delegation considered that insufficient use is being made of the weapon of information and propaganda. To some extent, the Mau Mau by using the traditional African channel of spreading rumours, the "bush telegraph" held the initiative in this field.

Mau Mau also used creative communications as a way of achieving their political and military aims. They forged symbols of colonialism to infiltrate enemy lines. Their members with special skills supported them in this. The Kenya Committee provides details and commentary, which provide a glimpse into this aspect of Mau Mau strategy:

- African tailor, making white arm bands similar to Homeguards, arrested. Bands used by freedom fighters as disguise. (Vol. 1, 07-04-1953, p.29)

- New emergency regulations making it an offence for anyone to wear naval, military, air force, police and other official uniforms without authorisation. (Vol.1, 29-05-1953, p.33).[33]

- A number of fishing boats operating from villages on the Kavirondo Gulf have been the subject of a report to the authorities. The name "Jomo Kenyatta" is painted on one boat, another bears the name, "Mau Mau". (Vol.1, 08-07-1955, p.151).

- The Kenya Government announced today that a Kikuyu woman who had been crowned "Mau Mau Queen" on Coronation Day, June 2, had been imprisoned for ten years for taking the Mau Mau oath and for being chair of a women's terrorist movement. (Vol.1, 02-01-1954).

---

33 This was in response to the tactics used by Mau Mau combatants to launch attacks wearing British army uniforms. Kinyatti (2002) records an event in 1953: "the KFLA unit disguised in enemy uniform ambushed a patrol of the KAR traitors at Ihuririo in Uthaya killing three of them".

Language of Resistance

The need for oral communication led to the development of a special language of resistance that only the liberation forces could understand. It thus became possible to pass on oral messages even in the presence of enemy forces and to use enemy controlled or censored newspapers for the same purpose. Even the colonial sources admitted the skilful use of such methods, as Leakey (1954) observes:

In view of the risk of written messages being intercepted by security forces, documentary methods were only seldom used [by the Mau Mau cadres], and when they were, they were nearly always so worded as to be seemingly innocuous.

To this end Mau Mau developed a most complex system of everyday words to indicate things other than what they seemed to mean and these code words were frequently changed. Examples of these code words are 'makara', which normally means charcoal, for ammunition; 'muti', which normally means a tree, for a gun; 'kamwaki', which means a little fire, for a revolver or pistol; and 'kihii', which means an overgrown boy, for a gunman.

Constant communication was maintained between the army in the forests and various councils at the upper level in Nairobi and elsewhere, responsible for collecting food, supplies, etc. [Additionally] an organisation was set up - mainly with women as couriers - to make and maintain contact with detained leaders in detention camps.

As a part of the arms business, it became necessary to have all sorts of special code words, so that the verbal and written messages could be sent about the (procuring), hiding, or distribution of firearms, that would be clear to the recipient, but not appear in the least suspicious to the ordinary security investigator.

Further examples of the development of language to suit the needs of waging an armed guerrilla movement are given by Barnett and Njama (1966), most of these dealing with military terms:

Banda	Guerrilla terminology for home-made guns
Bebeta	Derived from the Swahili term *pepeta*, meaning to winnow or sift. It was the guerrilla term for Stan gun.
Gatheci	Literally, 'sharp instrument'. It was the guerrilla term for Homeguard, derived from the fact that Homeguards were initially armed with spears.
Gathugo	Literally, 'throwing weapon'. Guerrilla term for Homeguard.
Gatimu	Literally, 'small spear'. Guerrilla term for Homeguard, derived from the fact that Homeguards were initially armed with spears.
Gatua uhoro	Literally, 'the decider'. Guerrilla term for big-game shooting guns ranging from .375 to .450.
Gicakuri	Singular of *icakuri*, meaning 'heavy pitchfork'. Guerrilla term for any government personnel or European.
Gikonyo	Protruding navel. Guerrilla term for British bombers, derived from the impression conveyed by the open bomb doors.
Ihii cia mititu	'Forest boys'. Guerrilla term for warriors.
Kamwaki	'Small fire'. Guerrilla term for pistol.
Kariiguru	'It is up'. Guerrilla term meaning that an air-plane was approaching.
Kenya Ng'ombe	Guerrilla term for (British) Kenya Regiment personnel, derived from the fact that Ng'ombe (cow) was the KR symbol.
Kuri hono-i ndirara?	A guerrilla signal to camp guards signifying that one was not an enemy.
Makara	'Charcoal'. Guerrilla term for ammunition.
Mbuci	Guerrilla terminology for a camp, derived from the English 'bush'.

Muhimu	A code term for the Mau Mau, meaning 'most important' in Kiswahili.
Muingi	"Community" or "people" (as opposed to "enemy"). A term used by the Mau Mau for workers and peasants.
Muirigo	'A clear forest path'.
Nakombora	'The destroyer'. Guerrilla term for Bren gun.
Nyagikonyo	'The bearer of a protruding navel'. Guerrilla term for the Lincoln heavy bomber.
Nyamu Nditu	'The heavy animal'. Guerrilla term for the Mau Mau.
Tie-Ties	African white collar worker; a pejorative term for Europeanised Africans who were least likely to assist in the revolutionary struggle for land and freedom. Refers to those who wore ties, a symbol of foreign culture.
The Townwatch Battalions	The guerrilla term for all those who fought in the towns, most of whom carried on their normal jobs during the day and fought at night.

Communication in Detention Camps

Mau Mau activists in detention camps developed the use of oral communications further. The living conditions were very harsh, and lack of proper food, poor housing conditions and hard labour made the lives of the inmates even more difficult. They were also deprived of contact with the outside world. No newspapers, radios or any news from outside the detention camp were allowed.

But the detainees developed their own oral news services and oral newspapers, with regular news, and were thus able to communicate with each other and to acquire news from outside detention centres about the struggle outside as well as world news. Kariuki (1975) describes some of these oral information services:

> In many ways the most important nourishment we had was from the two news services that we operated (at Manyani Detention Camp). The Manyani Times was the news that was known to be true which had been picked up from newspapers by those cleaning in the warder's lines or had been heard on a wireless by someone working near an officer's house. We were extremely cunning at obtaining news without being seen to do so.

> The Waya Times was the news that was largely speculation, rumours or light relief. In the evenings, after food, each 'club' in every compound would send a representative to the barbed wire partitions to get the news. We were extremely lucky in Compound 13 since we could converse with five other compounds. Anyone who had any news would stand up and say *giteo*, which is Kikuyu for 'respect' and brought instant silence all around him. Then he would say, "I now begin my words of Manyani Times (or Waya Times) which are that . . ." This immediately told his listeners how much credibility to place in what was coming. Waya Times news items might include the dismissal of the Governor, the date of Independence (never later than 1956), the revocation of unpleasant regulations by the Commissioner of Prisons, our imminent release...

> The warders disliked our news service intensely and whenever they saw us eagerly listening to it someone would throw a few stones to break us up. The evening news hour was also used for throwing tobacco to friends in other compounds.

Other detention camps also had similar communications network, for example the *Kamongo Times at* Saiyusi Detention Centre and *The Mukoma Times* at Lodwar Detention Centre. Pio Gama Pinto and Ramogi Achieng Oneko's contribution to the development of oral communications in detention camp is also significant. Oneko (1966) gives an interesting insight:

> [During detention on Manda Island] there came a time when the authorities had begun to engineer confusion in the camp in order to demoralise us. We realised that if we did not organise counter measures

and propaganda many of us (numbering about two hundred) would be wrecked. We therefore started a counter propaganda move. Pio was one of the editors and played a big role in a well organised network. It was his job to dish out information to the Lower Camp by word of mouth to our own propagandists. To the astonishment and surprise of the Camp Administration the morale of the detainees was restored and we remained hard and impenetrable.

It is noteworthy that the detention centres came to be known as "Mau Mau Universities" (Kenya Weekly News, 18-03-1955) as there was a well-developed programme run by experienced cadres to educate new inmates on the ideology and world outlook of Mau Mau. They also acted as recruitment grounds for new members.

McGhie (2002) reveals yet another use of oral tradition in detention camps as a form of resistance and records the brutality with which the colonial regime treated such resistance. The incident below took place at the Mwea detention centre:

> Mr Gavaghan explained, however, that there had, in past intakes, been more persistent resistors who had been forcibly changed into camp clothing. Some of them had started the 'Mau Mau howl', a familiar cry which was taken up by the rest of the camp, representing a concerted and symbolic defiance of the camp authorities. In such cases it was essential to prevent the infection of this 'oath' spreading throughout the camp, and the 'resistor' who started it was put on the ground, a foot placed on his throat and mud stuffed in his mouth. In the last resort, a man whose resistance could not be broken down was knocked unconscious. [34]

More information about such atrocities by the occupying British forces are coming into public domain as part of the war crimes inquiry launched by the Scotland Yard following the move by the Mau Mau veterans to start a potentially huge legal action for compensation for atrocities during the war of liberation.

Songs

Revolutionary songs were another aspect of Mau Mau's use of people's oral

---

[34]   McGhie (2002).

culture. They served a number of purposes. Songs became a powerful expression of people's culture in the struggle against colonial culture. They broke the colonial monopoly over means of communication and took the anti-colonial message right into people's homes. The content reflected the political needs of the struggle. Songs were tools of organising people against colonialism, a rallying point for people to identify with. They encouraged people to oppose a common enemy in an organised way and as a united force. Songs became a source of information and a record of history, which was passed on to the new generation.

New songs were made to record Mau Mau activities and events. For example, General Kariba's soldiers of the Kenya Levellation Army composed and sung songs to commemorate the battle of the Tumu Tumu Hill. Songs were used to propagate ideas about liberation, which could not be openly published due to colonialist censorship. Describing the 26th July 1952 KAU meeting at the Nyeri Show grounds, attended by over 30,000 people, Njama (Barnet and Njama, 1966) says:

> The organisation (Mau Mau) was given considerable publicity because most of the organisers of the meeting were Mau Mau leaders and most of the (audience), Mau Mau members. They were given the opportunity to circulate Mau Mau propaganda songs when both coming and leaving the meeting ... As I was pushing my bicycle uphill towards Muthuaini School where I was teaching I enjoyed many Mau Mau songs which were sung by the crowd as they left the meeting.

There were still other types of songs, the *Marari*, which were warrior songs encouraging the people to fight for their rights. The Mau Mau published many such songs when the movement began to spread over larger areas. One Mau Mau song was used by the Tamaduni Players (1978):

Utavumilia Kifo?
Watoto wa Kenya huishi mwituni
Wakinyeshewa na mvua
Wakipata njaa, mateso na baridi nyingi
Kwa upendo wa udongo.

Uui, iiyai, uui iiyai
Kuuawa na taabu na kufungwa
Mara nyingi
Je utavumilia?

Ni akina nani hao wanaimba kwa sauti kubwa
Ngambo ya pili ya mto
Wakiwaimbia Kago na Mbaria
Watafutaji wa haki.

Uui, iiyai, uui iiyai
Kuuawa na taabu na kufungwa
Mara nyingi
Je utavumilia?

Are you prepared to face death?
Sons and daughters of Kenya
Live in forests
Enduring thunder, starvation,
For the love of their soil.

Uui, iiyai, uui iiyai

Enduring torture and jailings
Time after time
Are you prepared?

And who are those
On the other side of the river
Singing in fearless voices
Praises and exploits of Kago and Mbaria
Seekers of our rights.

Uui, iiyai, uui iiyai
Enduring torture and jailings
Time after time
Are you prepared?

Kinyatti (2008) discusses the importance, purpose, and content of songs and oral medium as used by the Mau Mau. He identifies three aspects of oral communications, which developed during the changing contradictions of the times:

> Within a span of five years the Mau Mau produced most formidable political songs which were used as a weapon to politicise and educate the Kenyan worker and peasant masses. This helped heighten the people's consciousness against the forces of the foreign occupiers, and, in the process, prepared them for armed struggle. The role of these songs in educating the workers and peasants against the dictatorship of the colonialists was an undeniable catalyst in the development and success of the movement.

> [The second aspect] consisted of detention and prison songs from the early war years. They highlight the suffering in the camps and prisons. They express the people's bitterness against the "Homeguard" traitors who were hunting, spying on and torturing them in the camps and who superintended their eviction from the Settlers' plantations. The songs make it clear to these traitors that they will pay with their lives for their treachery. Some of them also eulogise the Mau Mau guerrillas in the forests of their heroism and express their confidence and faith in Field Marshall Dedan Kimaathi's leadership. Finally, they articulate the people's optimism that they will win the struggle against the forces of the occupation.

> [The third aspect consisted of] lyrics by guerrillas. One can sense the very flames of war in them. They glorify the revolutionary aspects of the Movement: its dialectical relationship with the worker and peasant masses on the one hand and its principal contradiction with British colonialism on the other.

One of the Mau Mau guerrilla songs reproduced by Kinyatti (1980) shows the freedom fighters' awareness of the sufferings of the people under colonialism; it mentions the fact that colonial laws were used to ban Kenyan newspapers; and the leadership's call "to unite and fight"; and the heroism of the people against the foreign enemy: the song is entitled *Declaration of War in Kenya*:

When the war was declared in 1952
Our country was turned into a huge prison.
Innocent people, men, women and children,
Were herded into concentration camps,
Under all kinds of harsh repression.

Our livestock were confiscated
And our crops in the fields were destroyed.
All public markets were closed down
And all people's newspapers were banned.

Meanwhile Kimaathi in Nyandarwa called for total mobilisation,
He told people to unite and fight
These foreign murderers with heroism
And drive them out of the country.

In spite of harsh enemy repression
The revolutionary flame was maintained and developed.
And people's hatred towards the British oppressors
Grew day by day,
And proudly they declared:
"It would be better to die on our feet
Than to live on our knees."

Many songs were written by Kinuthia wa Mugia, Muthee wa Cheche, Gakaara wa Wanjau, J. M. Kariuki, Karari wa Wanjau, and Mohamed Mathu. These songs were then circulated to people as orature. Many were also printed and published as booklets by activist organisations such as Gakaara Book Service. An example of a songbook is *Witikio*, which became extremely popular. Others were printed and distributed as individual cyclostyled sheets.

The effectiveness of the oral sources of information was proven when the highest level of confidential British information reached the Mau Mau before it became public knowledge. This happened, for example, when the colonial government declared a State of Emergency. The news had already reached the combatants through the organisation's well-placed activists, even before an official announcement was made. The Kenya Committee Press Extracts (1952, Vol.1 pp. 6-7) records the events:

> On Monday, October 20th, the State of Emergency was declared...over 100 African leaders were arrested...There was one hitch however in the Government's elaborate plans. News of the impending arrests leaked out causing the Government to advance the arrests by one hour. In spite of this advancement, many Africans on the list for arrest were warned in time to make their escape – most likely to the forests!

This was also the case when the colonial authorities made a surrender offer to Mau Mau in 1955. The London *Times* (17-01-1955) expresses colonial frustration at the ease with which information reached Mau Mau combatants before it was officially sent:

> In both cases, as now, there has been a breach of security, and the news of the impending offer has leaked out ahead of schedule. The fact that such leakages can still occur scarcely inspires confidence in the ability of the authorities to handle these surrender offers in the best circumstances.

Publishing

Revolutionary publishing of this period was aimed at satisfying the communication needs of the guerrilla army to maintain links among themselves, as well as with the masses which provided it support. Three different levels of publishing activities were used in keeping with the particular conditions of the time. These were:

1. The use of existing 'legal' newspapers which were sympathetic to the Movement to pass on their messages to the people and to receive intelligence reports through coded messages.

2. The establishment of many new publications which functioned 'legally' for a time before the colonial government suppressed them. Others would then

be started to replace the suppressed ones.

3. The third level was the establishment of Mau Mau's own publishing industry with its own printing works, editors, reporters and technical experts. They developed a network of printing presses in liberated and semi liberated areas, which were under the control of the people's forces. An independent distribution network supplemented this.

"Legal" Publications

"Legal" publications were newspapers, books and other printed material, which were published under colonial laws. The colonial government was not, however, aware of the real purpose served by these publications. Although the intelligence branch of the colonial police censored these publications very strictly, the liberation forces managed to pass on much information to its supporters and also used them to create anti-colonial consciousness among people. An example is the use of *Mumenyereri* to pass on messages about anti-imperialist meetings to its supporters under the guise of "tea parties".

These 'legal' publications developed in contradiction to the colonial controlled publications. Specifically they helped the liberation forces to counter colonial propaganda broadcast over radio stations, newspapers, books and educational systems. It was the specific conditions of this period which shaped the publishing activities.

It is important to realise the close co-operation during this period between progressive South Asian press workers and their African counterparts on the liberation front. Spencer (1983) records their contribution:

> ...There were other Indians (besides Apa Pant) who did even more but whose importance has been overlooked. These were the men in the newspaper business: printers, publishers, and editors, whose machines produced the African papers. It would be difficult to overstate the significance of these new publications...all these papers helped build a political awareness that had not existed before. Because European printers obviously would not touch them and since, for several years after the War, no African could afford to publish them on their own, it

was left to the Indians … to print these new African papers.

The use of the existing publications was one way in which the revolutionary forces communicated with their supporters. Mau Mau did not control these but they managed to use whatever openings there were to pass on their messages through the columns of local papers. But given that they controlled a large administrative machinery which had jurisdiction over vast areas with hundreds of thousands of people, other methods of communication had to be developed.

One such method used by Mau Mau was the establishment of 'legal' newspapers. This was possible in the late 1940s and early 1950s. By 1954, about fifty such newspapers were established by the liberation forces. As soon as the colonial administration became aware of the reality that Mau Mau controlled them, they were banned.   Most of these were in one of the nationality languages or in Kiswahili and supported Mau Mau and the independence movement.   They were in fact, directly or indirectly, controlled by the Mau Mau High Command through its Mathare Valley headquarters in Nairobi. Some of these are listed in Durrani, S. (2006).

Newspapers were started by Mau Mau for political reasons, to give publicity to their political demands and to organise the masses behind Mau Mau ideology and programme. Mass meetings organised by KAU were becoming very popular with thousands attending. One way in which the colonial administration tried to stop these meetings was to cut off any publicity for them. The European-owned newspapers would not report these meetings and there thus developed an information gap, which needed to be addressed by Mau Mau. It did so by launching a number of newspapers in nationality languages, all indirectly controlled by the High Command and run by individuals who were not known by the government as belonging to Mau Mau.   Thus the organisation was protected from being known by the colonial administration and even when many newspapers were banned, the organisation remained intact.

Among papers started by activists were: *Inooro ria Gikuyu* (November 1951), *Afrika Mpya* (October 1952), *Gikuyu na Mumbi, Wihuge,* and *Wiyathi*. There were many songbooks, such as *Witikio*, all of which were spreading the same message. They gave a political interpretation to events and also publicised KAU activities.

Around this time, the old contradictions between the two ways of achieving independence sharpened. On the one hand were those who favoured petitioning the colonial government to 'grant' independence; on the other hand were those who maintained that the only way to remove imperialism from Kenya was through an armed struggle. The latter started preparations for an armed struggle soon after 1945 and represented the worker consciousness of the Kenyan proletariat. It was this line which merged with militant nationalists and trade unionists to become Mau Mau.

Kaggia (1975) records the conditions of the time:

> My newspapers and the others founded during 1951 and 1952, catered for politically conscious readers. It was the period of great strides in oath administration; it was a period of change, when people were beginning to lose their faith in gradual constitutional progress. Many young initiates were very impatient. They were always asking when we were going to take up arms and fight for our rights. The newspaper editors had to write for this audience, even if it meant being prosecuted. We had only one aim: to arouse people to the point where they would be ready to do anything for Kenya. We didn't consider our own safety or welfare.

The activities of the African press had begun to worry the colonial authorities as early as 1946 from which time they sought to find ways, legal or otherwise, to suppress Kenyan publishing. A meeting of provincial commissioners held on 26th October, 1946 discussed the issue of newspapers and recommended that the following points be sent to the Secretary of State in Britain as recorded by Corfield (1960):

> · That the present trend of the [African] press constituted a grave menace to the future of the Colony.

> · That certain [African] newspapers were being financed and influenced by seditious minded Indians and that their object was purely anti-government and anti-European.

> · That, as regards freedom of the press, liberty was being mistaken for licence, and that in addition to deliberate distortion of facts, many of the articles in such newspapers contained a most dangerous and

pernicious form of anti-European propaganda.

· Asking for information as to what legislation existed in any other British Colony for the control of the Press, and suggesting consideration of the possibility of some form of supervision or censorship.

In the following months, even more local publications emerged and the message they carried became even more anti-imperialist and militant, demanding even more urgent changes. The colonialists' concern was voiced by the Acting Chief Native Commissioner to the Member for Law and Order and the Deputy Chief Secretary on 20th February, 1947, quoted in Corefield (1960):

In my view the general tone of these tribal newspapers since the date of the provincial commissioners' meeting in October last year has steadily deteriorated and the situation which was urgent enough then is worse today. As you are aware, 18 months ago there was practically no (national) Press, with the exception of the *Baraza*, which is run by the East African Standard and which is, broadly speaking, moderate in tone. Since that date a number of newspapers edited by Africans and published in English, Swahili, and the vernacular languages has sprung up ... To my mind a serious cause of this cleavage is the continuous stream of lies, misrepresentation and colour consciousness which is pouring out from vernacular presses, and which is inspired by a few Africans, abetted by the owners of the Indian presses who produce these papers. In my view, if we are unable to control this unpleasant stream, we are bound to have trouble in this Colony, and I do not think it is going too far to say that those troubles may well lead to bloodshed. If we are to avoid trouble, we have got to fight this deliberate attempt to drive a wedge between the African peoples and the Europeans in this country.

Thus the liberation forces faced the enemy not only on the battlefield; the powerful enemy propaganda machinery kept up a continuous attack to misrepresent the national struggle. The cause of the freedom fighters and their supporters was deliberately distorted by the colonial propaganda. This presented Mau Mau as a 'savage atavistic movement'. The 1950s was a period of war of independence in Kenya, but the colonial administration presented the events as acts of barbarism, as happened in all anti colonial wars. Odinga (1968) takes up the aspect of colonial propaganda against Mau Mau:

> The sensational anti-Mau Mau propaganda of the period is a gross insult to the leadership of Dedan Kimathi and the brave men he led who defied death in a guerrilla army for the freedom cause in Kenya.

> The propaganda against the Mau Mau as a "savage atavistic movement" – from sensational press reports, to government and army handouts and the British Government Corfield Commission – was so fierce…The Emergency was a time of revolutionary war in Kenya. For almost a decade in the fifties only one side in this battle was able to present its case and its account of events.

For its part, the Kenya Parliament, established by the liberation forces, continued to interpret events from the point of view of Kenyan masses and made it very clear what the fight against imperialism was all about (Odinga, 1968):

> We are fighting for all land stolen from us by the [British] Crown through its Orders in Council of 1915, according to which Africans have been evicted from the Kenya Highlands. The British Government must grant Kenya full independence under African leadership, and hand over all land previously alienated for distribution to the landless. We will fight until we achieve freedom or until the last of our warriors has shed their last drop of blood.

Dedan Kimathi explained in a letter, quoted by Odinga (1968) he wrote from his headquarters in Nyandarua in 1955 to the Nairobi newspaper *Habari za Dunia* that "the poor are the Mau Mau. Poverty can be stopped, but not by bombs and weapons from the imperialists. Only the revolutionary justice of the struggles of the poor can end poverty for Kenyans".

The Mau Mau High Command gave much importance to the communications aspect of the struggle. As Barnet and Njama (1966) record, in January 1955, when a secret meeting was held to make important organisational changes, various committees were formed with one of them being made responsible for information and publishing. The secret War Council, which had the overall responsibility for co-ordinating political and military activities, had its headquarters at Mathare in Nairobi in the mud and thatch houses among the trees. It was here that Mau Mau publishing and printing activities were located and from where its national publicity was organised.

The early period of active revolutionary anti-imperialist war saw the build-up of armed forces, which assumed control over a large part of the country. We saw earlier how some areas in Nairobi came under full control of the liberation forces. Many people like Corfield had to admit that by August, 1952, in large parts of Central Province which was the primary battlefield, colonial law and law courts "had virtually ceased to function." [35] Their functions were taken over by Mau Mau revolutionary courts, which established justice for workers and peasants and carried out sentences against colonial officers, saboteurs and other anti-people elements. Thus between May and October, 1952 (*before* the Declaration of Emergency) Homeguard comprador traitors including Chief Waruhiu had been sentenced by Mau Mau courts and the sentences carried out by the armed liberation forces.

It was in this atmosphere that Mau Mau established over fifty newspapers, which were all banned by the colonial government using the 'emergency' powers after 1952.

Intelligence Gathering and Communications

Mau Mau organised an efficient intelligence-gathering system right from the beginning of the struggle. It was only later that the colonial regime came to realise the full extent of this system.

Collecting information was only one aspect of intelligence work; another was ensuring that information was available to the Central Command and to the fighting units. This was also organised by Mau Mau. One of the most important methods was through oral communication, which was the safest, given the increased enemy surveillance activities. It was based on the orature developed over many generations by the people. This led to the development of a special language that only the patriotic forces could understand. Thus it became possible to pass on oral messages even in the presence of enemy soldiers, or to pass on written messages using enemy-controlled newspapers.

---

35 Corfield (1960), p. 279.

Not only was a constant communication system maintained between the Army in the forest and the various Councils at the upper level in Nairobi and elsewhere that were responsible for collecting food, supplies etc. An organisation was also set up - mainly with women as couriers - to make and maintain contact with detained leaders in detention camps.

Paul Maina (1977) explains the working of the Kenda Kenda Organisation set up by Mau Mau for its intelligence gathering activities:

> For the purpose of concealing Mau Mau activities in Nairobi and elsewhere an elaborate intelligence service called the Kenda Kenda (Nine Nine) Organisation was formed. This consisted of (people) from all walks of life in and around Nairobi. Its agents were the taxi drivers, European house servants, men working in big government offices and even beggars who sat at street corners all day. All information of value was passed on to the Kenda Kenda Organisation and then to the Central Committee. As a result of the success of the Kenda Kenda, Mau Mau activities went undetected in Nairobi until late in 1952.

Another aspect of information work was that of dealing with the training of cadres who would undertake politicisation work among the masses. This was an essential part of Mau Mau's work as without it, it would be difficult to continue receiving the people's support in their work. At the same time, it helped to train cadres who would assume important work in the years to come. Kaggia (1975) explains the importance of this work:

> Other active groups of young men and women played equally important roles in our organisation and recruitment. These were the propagandists who went round telling people about the aims of the movement and selling our literature. Besides newspapers like *Inooro ria Gikuyu*, *Gikuyu na Mumbi*, *Wihuge*, *Wiyathi* and others, there were the many song books, such as *Witikio*, all of which were spreading the same message. All these had to be advertised and sold. Through the work of these dedicated people, as they dispensed literature and organised (national) dances, many young people who would otherwise have been uninterested in politics were brought into our movement.

So important was this work of distribution of political books and politicisation of the masses that many Mau Mau leaders had at one time or another undertaken it. Kimathi himself had been involved in it. This was in connection with the distribution of *Witikio wa Gikuyu na Mumbi* which was published by Gakara wa Wanjau, who was detained by the Colonial regime from 1952 to 1959. Gakara recently recalled how his publications passed from hand to hand under the cover of darkness in the jungle among the guerrilla fighters and in cities and towns. One such publication was *Witikio* with its message of inalienable land rights of the people. It was printed on a four page card and was selling at twenty five cents each. It was intended only for those who had taken the oath of unity. It was this publication which Kimathi helped distribute. This was in the months of September and October 1952, when the Colonial administration declared a state of Emergency. At this time, Kimathi managed to take about 15,000 copies of *Witikio* in large baskets to the Rift Valley people within a period of two weeks.

Leadership

All the aspects of governance, the actual conduct of warfare, the political aspects of Kenya Parliament and other actions mentioned above were not spontaneous acts happening in a political, social and military vacuum. There was a guiding force behind them all. And that force was Mau Mau leadership, which is often ignored or minimised by historical studies. Mau Mau leadership needs to be seen in a dynamic level in all its aspects.

It is not possible to see Mau Mau leadership in the sense that one sees the leader of a Western country personalised in the person of a president or a prime minister. The reality of fighting, with limited resources, against the superpower dictated that a different model of leadership had to be found if the movement was to succeed. At the same time, the War of Independence in Kenya was not directed by an organised political party as happened in Mozambique under FRELIMO or in Namibia under SWAPO. As seen earlier, forces in Kenya were coming together to form such a political-military organisation before British colonial government pre-empted the development with its excessive use of force under the guise of an emergency. Of necessity, Kenya's War of Independence was led and organised in a way that suited local conditions.

At the same time, as seen earlier, there were a number of aspects that came together to form the various strands of the War of Independence. These included the trade union movement, the nationalistic forces active over a long period, the peasant movements that had a long history of anti-colonialist struggles as well as members of public including taxi drivers, publishers, doctors and lawyers, not organised as trade unions but acting in sympathy with progressive forces. All these specific forces of resistance had their own leadership in terms of organisation and individual leaders. In a broad sense these gave organisational, ideological and individual leadership to the War of Independence. A comprehensive history of Kenya's War of Independence would probe the leadership at all these levels.

It has become customary in history under capitalism to see leaders only as those who stand at the top of political movements and parties. Whereas the reality in movements such as Mau Mau and Kenya's War of independence was that there was leadership at every level of organisation, with the smallest unit of organisation having its own leaders. Thus at the level of trade unions, shop stewards led many strikes in Kenya and were thus leaders in their own right. So were the leaders of the unions as a whole, with the overall body such as the East African Trade Union Congress leaders forming a national umbrella body of trade unions.

The same can be said about Mau Mau. While Kimathi and other leaders in the forest were no doubt leaders of the movement, it is not possible to ignore leaders at divisions, provinces and cell levels who propelled the movement. It is appropriate to see history in terms of the spirit of the question posed by Brecht (1935):

Questions From a Worker Who Reads
Who built Thebes of the 7 gates?
In the books you will read the names of kings.
Did the kings haul up the lumps of rock?

And Babylon, many times demolished,
Who raised it up so many times ?

In what houses of gold glittering Lima did its builders live?

Where, the evening that the Great Wall of China was finished, did the
masons go?

Great Rome is full of triumphal arches.
Who erected them?

Over whom did the Caesars triumph?

Had Byzantium, much praised in song, only palaces for its inhabitants?

Even in fabled Atlantis, the night that the ocean engulfed it,
The drowning still cried out for their slaves.

The young Alexander conquered India.
Was he alone?

Caesar defeated the Gauls.
Did he not even have a cook with him?

Philip of Spain wept when his armada went down.
Was he the only one to weep?

Frederick the 2nd won the 7 Years War.
Who else won it?

Every page a victory.
Who cooked the feast for the victors?

Every 10 years a great man.
Who paid the bill?

So many reports.
So many questions.

Leadership of the complex War of Independence in Kenya, if it is to do justice
to every level of leadership, is a vast topic that needs to be examined in much
greater detail than is possible within the scope of this book. At the same time,
those who planned, fought and died in the course of the war cannot be forgotten.

Kaggia, B.Leeum, and Kaggia, M (2012) mention a few leaders whose records need to be written fully:

> Besides Dedan Kimathi, whose leadership and influence kept the war going all the time, a number of truly great soldiers distinguished themselves by any war standards. I will mention only a few: Stanley Mathenge, Gitau Matenjagwo, Ihura Kareri, Manyeki Wangombe, Kago Mboko, Mbaria Kaniu and Waruhiu Itote. These men were greatly revered by their fellow Mau Mau soldiers and by all Africans in general. They were feared by the British Government soldiers and their helpers.

Leaders such the ones mentioned above are essential in any social movement. Without them, Mau Mau could not have fought the strongest force in the world.

A Movement of All People

One of the long-term and intense damaging effects that colonialism engineered in Kenya – as in other places such as India – is the creation of artificial antagonistic divisions among people based on issues that had not divided people before colonialism. One such division was ethnic differences, which were not antagonistic but were rendered so by colonialism's "tribal" policies. Other divisions that colonialism used were based on regions, religions and gender. Capitalism was to add a yet more divisive factor along class lines.

Colonialism faced a united opposition of all the people and nationalities to its rule. It had no weapons in its arsenal to face people's demand for liberation. Its strategy of dealing with this opposition was "divide and rule" which it had used in other parts of the world. Furedi (1989) explains this further:

> Although the administrators of Kenya were consummate practitioners of the policy of divide and rule, ethnicity only emerges as a political factor in the 1950s. In the White Highlands, an area of heterogeneous ethnic mix, there is evidence of ethnic identification throughout the period under consideration. However, it is only in the late 1950s that tribalism emerges as an important political influence.

> The evidence from our investigation suggests that tribalism is not the natural

or inevitable consequence of ethnic identification. In the case of Kenya, a tribalist consciousness was strengthened through the implementation of policies designed to fragment nationalist politics. The expulsion of Kikuyu squatters became an invitation for other ethnic groups to take their place. When Kikuyu squatters returned to the White Highlands they were portrayed as intruders on the welfare of other ethnic groups. These local tensions were part of a national pattern. What colonial policies achieved was to create the impression that the interests of one ethnic group could only be enforced at the expense of another.

It is therefore important to see Kenya's War of Independence as a movement of all the people for liberation and not to fall into the colonial traps of artificial hostile divisions created by imperialism. This section looks at some aspects of people's unity in the war of independence.

The need for instruments of governance mentioned earlier implied that Mau Mau controlled the lives and territories of people in large parts of the country. The Kenyan War of Independence, led by Mau Mau, was a national movement for liberation. It served British colonial interests to present the movement as a tribal one and create the myth that it was not a national movement in which many nationalities participated. Nor did they want to show the reality of the involvement of workers from all nationalities and the trade union movement. While it is true that not every part of the country participated equally actively in the active stages of the struggle, this is by no means unique to Kenya. Resistance develops from small sparks where the pain of colonial exploitation is the greatest and where the oppressed people are in a position to struggle actively. However, it served British interests to further divide Kenyan people into the so-called Mau Mau and non-Mau Mau on the basis of those who fought for independence and those who did not. Yet evidence suggests many nationalities were active in the struggle. For example, Edgerton (1990):

> When Kenyatta said that "we all fought for Uhuru," he was repeating a politically expedient slogan, not a fact. Still, in reality many more Kenyans gave their support to Mau Mau and its call for freedom than the government liked, or wanted the world to realise. Information relating to the spread of Mau Mau was classified, and although some of it leaked to the press, the magnitude of the threat was not known to the public.

Mau Mau attacks now took place anywhere in Kenya from Mombasa to Kisumu on Lake Victoria. While the spread of Mau Mau was indeed a threat to the colonial power and its local supporters, it was no threat to the majority of Kenyans who had nothing to lose but their colonised status. This brief section gives just a few examples of some groups who participated in the War of Independence. A complete history on this aspect also needs to be researched and written.

Illustrations 3: Mau Mau

Dedan Kimathi

Kavote and Peter Nthirima in 1963

Kenya Resist No. 1

SAUTI YA KAMUKUNJI

INSIDE

- University Workers - N.S.S.F. Deduction
- Where to From Campus?
- Maji Maji Rebellion
- Workers Corner
- Is SONU dying a Natural Death?
- Jailed Students Fund Lauched

General Kago

Field Marshal Dedan Kimathi

General Kariba

Muthoni Kirima

Mbaria Kaniu

Karari Njama

Field Marshal Mutungi

Kavote

from their sources of supply and support in the reserves. *Below*: A Lincoln heavy bomber on a raid over the Aberdares. Photos: Kenya Information Services

Emergency Village

Travelling in long convoys of vehicles under tight Screening and Detention Camp

Security suspect arrive at the screening and possible
Detention Camp

Field Marshal
Mwariama
N'Kirigua, 1963

Warrant of Commitment on
a Sentence of Imprisonment
or Fine.

CRIMINAL No. 102

COLONY AND PROTECTORATE OF KENYA

In the .... SUPREME .... Court

at .... NYERI. ....

To the Superintendent of Prison,

N.Y.E.R.I.

WHEREAS on ...... 27th ...... day of .... November, ... 195..6

...... DEDAN KIMATHI S/O WACHIURI ......
(Name of prisoner)

the (............) Prisoner in Criminal Case No. 46

of 195.6 was convicted before me .. Sir Kenneth O'Connor, Chief Justice
(Name and official designation)

H.M. SUPREME COURT OF KENYA of the offence of .. Unlawful possession
(Mention the offence briefly)

of ammunitions

.... under Section Regulation 8A (1A) of the
Emergency Regulations 1952

and was sentenced to, Imprisonment for ..... Seven (7)

Years with Hard Labour

This is to authorize and require you, the said Superintendent, to receive the said
.... DEDAN KIMATHI S/O WACHIURI ....
(Prisoner's name)

into your custody in the said jail, together with this warrant, and there carry the
aforesaid sentence into execution according to law.

Given under my hand and the Seal of the Court this ...... 27th ......

day of ..... November, ... 195.6

K. K. O'Connor.

Chief Justice,
H.M. Supreme Court of Kenya.
(P.T.O

ENDORSEMENT

I have the honour to inform you that I carried out the sentence of death upon

.... DEDAN KIMATHI S/O WACHIURI. ....

in the Prison at ..NAIROBI........................ at 6,........... a.m. this 18th,...........

day of .....February,.............. 19 57...

....
Superintendent of the Prison.

I hereby certify that I was present at the execution of ..DEDAN KIMATHI S/O WACHIURI.

at about 6 a.m,...... this morning and .... after

the execution I examined the body of the deceased man and found life to be extinct. Death

was caused by ..HANGING........................ and was * ..INSTANTANEOUS,...........

Dated at ..NAIROBI............... this 18th,........ day of .....February,

19 57...

K. E. ROBERTSON
....
Medical Officer.

* Instantaneous.

copy to—

The Hon. Chief Secretary,Nairobi.
The Registrar Supreme Court of Kenya,Nairobi.
The Commissioner of Prisons,Nairobi.

The Final Stage: Battles Lost, Battles Won

The two opposing forces engaged in the War of Independence were, on the one hand, the British army, navy and air force - the most powerful superpower in the world at the time; on the other hand were Kenyan people's forces with limited armaments, some stolen from their enemies, some basic ones manufactured by themselves in make-shift factories. However, they were armed with total commitment to "die on their feet" while seeking the return of their land and freedom. The question is whether or not they succeeded in their aims.

Kaggia, B., Leeuw and M. Kaggia (2012) record the achievements of Mau Mau as fighters:

> In the battle Mau Mau soldiers distinguished themselves as great guerrilla fighters. General Sir George Erskine, a British general, advised his Government that Mau Mau could not be stamped out by force. Although the General was soon to be removed from command, what he said was true and the Government eventually had to accept it in practice. The British couldn't crash Mau Mau with all their sophisticated weapons. Considering the difficult conditions under which the Mau Mau soldiers fought and lived, it is impossible to ignore their greatness. They managed to fight the war for more than four years. Besides Dedan Kimathi, whose leadership and influence kept the war going all the time, a number of truly great soldiers distinguished themselves by any war standards. I will mention only a few: Stanley Mathenge, Gitau Matenjagwo, Ihuru Kareri, Manyeki Wangombe, Kago Mboko, Mbaria Kaniu and Waruhiu Itote. These men were greatly revered by their fellow Mau Mau soldiers and by all Africans in general. They were feared by the British Government soldiers and their helpers.

A fuller understanding of the battles and their impact can perhaps emerge once all the recently released "lost" files of the British Government are analysed. Yet the picture is by no means unclear. Newsinger (2006) gives figures of casualties on both sides of the conflict:

> The official British figure of rebels killed in action was 11,503, but the real figure was much higher. Some estimates go as high as 50,000, and this is much closer to the truth. The casualties suffered by the [British]

security forces were considerably lower: only 12 European soldiers and 52 European police were killed, three Asians and 524 African soldiers and police. ... as for settler casualties, only 32 were killed in the course of the emergency, less than died in traffic accidents in Nairobi in the same period. What was successfully portrayed by the British government as a pogrom against the white Settlers was in fact a pogrom against the Kikuyu.

This excludes civilian suffering in Kenya. Again, Newsinger (2006) provides further insight:

Unofficial repression was accompanied by the most ferocious repression. As well as tens of thousands interned without trial (the best estimate is that over 160,000 people were interned during the course of the emergency), even more were imprisoned for emergency offences. Between 1952 and 1958 over 34,000 women were to be imprisoned for Mau Mau offences, and the number of men imprisoned was probably ten times that figure. According to one historian [Anderson, 2005], "at least one in four Kikuyu adult males was imprisoned or detained by the British colonial administration.

But this was not the end of the story, as Dowden (2005) records:

But the British also deployed an even more fatal if effective method, the one they had used against Afrikaner civilians in the Boer war, the concentration camp. Both Anderson and Elkins draw convincing parallels with Nazi concentration camps and Stalin's gulags. More than one million people were crammed into heavily guarded camps where starvation and disease killed thousands.

On the outside, the army used the same tactics that the Sudanese government has been using against the rebels in Darfur: they armed the local enemies of the rebellion and encouraged them to kill, rape and loot at will. When accounts of British atrocities leaked out, officials in Nairobi and London lied to deny them. When a few brave souls spoke out or even resigned, they were persuaded to keep quiet. When at last some of the truth came out the game was up.

These examples of colonial brutality were not an unintended outcome of a dirty war, nor "collateral damage" of a larger war. It was an integral part of a well-planned strategy, as *Hunting the Mau Mau* (2013) confirms:

> Other measures included the setting up of controlled villagers as a punitive measure against areas suspected of being solidly behind the Mau Mau. By early 1955 over a million Kikuyu had been settled in these villages.

Such brutality was the norm from the earliest days of European colonialism in Africa. And the global records of slavery, elimination of native people, the looting and confiscation of people's land and property are all parts of the same picture of how colonialism and imperialism shaped the lives of people around the world. Tharoor (2016) explores the colonial looting and brutality in India. The experience in China and other countries is no different. Kenya's is but a small part of a global picture of colonial and imperialist plunder, looting, massacres and "sinning quietly".

Mau Mau and their supporters made many sacrifices in their struggle to achieve Kenya's independence. They were shown no humanity nor given a peaceful way of addressing their concerns. Brutality, economic strangulations, massacres and torture were the response of the occupying colonial government. The occupiers eventually lost out by having to give in to demands for independence; yet they won in the long run by ensuring that imperialism flourished in Kenya. Mau Mau won the moral, and belatedly, the legal battle. In this they were not the first, nor will they be the last resistance movements against colonialism and imperialism. The battles may be over, but the wars of total liberation rage on - in Kenya as elsewhere in the world.

There are lessons to be learnt from the Kenyan War of Independence - for Kenyans as well as for people around the world: how did the resistance movement survive so long against the vastly superior military machinery of British colonialists and how were they finally side-lined? The defeat of France and USA in Vietnam taught its own lessons on people's struggle for liberation. Kenya stands proudly in the long list of "teachers of liberation".

Forces of Repression

Following the declaration of a state of war (officially called the "Emergency") by the colonial authorities in October 1952, the stage of armed resistance began in earnest. The guerrilla forces established their new military headquarters in the forests from where the armed battles were planned and executed. Many small and large guerrilla units had entered the forests and waged battles against the enemy in their local areas. It is to the credit of Mau Mau that it recognised the need to co-ordinate the activities of these different fighting units and to form an umbrella military organisation that could control the overall strategy of warfare in the face of a well-armed and equipped enemy.

It is useful to see the strength of British forces that Mau Mau had to confront. Too often Mau Mau is seen in isolation as if they were fighting some unseen, imaginary force in the sky. This robs them of an acknowledgement of their achievement of fighting a major superpower of the day. A brief look at British strategy and military strength can provide a better perspective on the Kenyan War of Independence. The strength of the British forces in 1953 is recorded by Barnett and Njama (1966):

> To implement this new offensive strategy, [British] security force strength was greatly increased and, by September [1953], included 39th Brigade of Buffs and Devons, the 49th Brigade of Royal Northumberland and Inniskilling Fusiliers, the East African Brigade of six KAR [Kenya African Rifles] battalions, the Lancashire Fusiliers, the Kenya Regiment and two East African units, an armoured car division and a squadron of Lincolns – a total of eleven battalions and over 10,000 soldiers. In addition, the police force was increased to 21,000 men and the Kikuyu guard units to a somewhat higher figure. During the third quarter of 1953, then, the British and Kenya Governments were employing a force of well over 50,000 men against the Mau Mau insurgents.

Barnett and Njama (1966) mention the use by the British forces of bombing by Harvard and Lincoln bombers and recount the effects of 1,000 lb. bombs dropped on Mau Mau combatants and the countryside. The tactics used by the British armed forces were the tried and tested ones all around the Empire. "Hunting the Mau Mau" website provides some useful insight on the strength and tactics used:

> The British forces in Kenya employed the tried and tested tactics which had worked so well in the counter-insurgency operations in Malaya. The problem was to balance the wealth of knowledge with the flexibility of response, allowing the knowledge of past experience to meld with what was needed in the theatre, but not to rigidly apply that knowledge to the exclusion of ingenuity and individual experience. This knowledge dates back to the Boer War and beyond to colonial operations ... In the British army's war against Mau Mau it was evident from the start that both branches of the government were agreed that "Mau Mau had to be suppressed; political negotiations were totally inconceivable."

The website goes on to record the strength of the British armed forces lined up against Mau Mau:

After the declaration of the State of Emergency it soon became clear that the colonial government had no strategy for dealing with the revolt and unrest. The governor requested and obtained British and African troops including the King's African Rifles. The troops were composed of:

1st Lancashire Fusiliers (from the Canal Zone)
4th KAR (from Uganda)
6th KAR (from Tanganyika)
Local KAR Battalions

The site also provides details of British forces under Royal Air Force, Army, Royal Navy and local forces. It will thus be seen that the Mau Mau forces were so well organised that all branches of the British armed forces had to be mobilised in order to defeat them. Newsinger (2006) sums up the balance of forces during this period:

> The [white] Settlers dreamed of a permanent white supremacist regime in Kenya ... Mau Mau, however, had shown that the Settlers did not have the strength to survive on their own. Without the British government

coming to their assistance in the 1950s, Mau Mau would have won.

When the armed stage began in 1952, Mau Mau maintained over 35,000 active fighters in the forests, and many thousands more in urban areas. It maintained friendly relations with thousands of peasants and workers. Its influence extended over a large part of the country, from Mombasa on the Coast to Kisumu in western Kenya. It even extended over parts of Tanganyika (now mainland Tanzania) where the British authorities were forced to declare a state of Emergency in Northern Tanganyika at the same time as it was declared over Kenya.

As one of Mau Mau struggle songs, "we are everywhere" (Maina, P., 1977) made clear, the presence of the guerrilla forces was felt everywhere:

If you go to Nairobi

We are there.

If you go to Mombasa,

We are there.

And if you go to Kisumu

We are there.

We are so many

That we are everywhere.

These facts indicate that the Mau Mau must have had a vast organisational network to be able to keep the large British military machinery on the run.

Mau Mau faced defeat not at the hands of British colonial forces, but at the hands of the government of an independent Kenya led by Jomo Kenyatta, which took over this responsibility in the interest of imperialism. But the colonial administration ensured it provided ample ammunition to the Kenyatta government to fulfil this task successfully. Angelo (2017), for example, records one aspect of this support:

Most of the prominent members of Kenyatta's government were selected and trained within colonial administrative system (re)shaped during the Emergency, and part and parcel of the Mau Mau counter-insurgency.

Those who were appointed provincial commissioners at independence had been trained by T. J. F. Gavaghan, the brains behind the brutal rehabilitation politics during the Mau Mau war and later appointed in 1961 as training officer of the Kenyan provincial administration. By 1965, two top members of the Office of the President were renowned loyalists: Duncan Ndegwa (Permanent Secretary) and Jeremiah Kiereini Under-Secretary in charge of the provincial administration.

That was only one aspect of the Kenyatta Government's efforts in attacking Mau Mau. A more brutal approach was the elimination of Mau Mau leadership, reminiscent of the worst excesses of colonialism, as Angelo (2017) shows:

Around the time of independence (1961–1965), Kenya's African nationalist government organized the continued repression of the remaining Mau Mau fighters who had refused to surrender after the ending of the Emergency in January 1960. [One such case focused] on Meru district, in Eastern Province, where Mau Mau fighters gathered under the leadership of Field Marshalls Mwariama and Baimungi. Documents from the Kenyan National Archives, in particular the correspondence of the provincial administration and security reports, show that politicians and officials alike saw the remaining fighters in Meru as a potent political threat to the nationalist government of Jomo Kenyatta. Kenya's government sought to deal with the Mau Mau threat by co-opting its leaders, while Kenyatta carefully distanced the presidency from the government's choice of repressive politics. A symbolic propaganda campaign was organized to maintain the myth that Kenyatta had always been the Mau Mau leader the British arrested and jailed in 1953, despite the reality of Kenyatta's repeated denunciation of the movement. After 1963, the President continued to ignore Mau Mau fighters' fundamental claims over land redistribution... the Kenya government organized a violent repression of Mau Mau in order to deprive freedom fighters of their leaders and to force them to retreat into silence.

Among the leaders killed were Field Marshall Baimungi and Chui "believed to be the most dangerous leaders" (Angelo, 2017), both "killed by police in a dawn swoop on the forest"[36]

---

36   *Daily Nation,* 27-01-1965, quoted by Angelo, 2017.

Primary Aim

The primary aim of the War of Independence - as the name suggests - was independence for Kenya. And that aim was achieved. Without an armed struggle, Kenya's independence would have been delayed at best, and the European Settlers would have increased their power and perhaps even been granted independence on their own terms. The Settlers in Southern Rhodesia achieved such a "victory" after its Universal Declaration of Independence in 1965. That singular achievement of Mau Mau tends to be ignored in colonial interpretation of Kenyan history. The comprador regime after independence accepted this version of Kenya's history and saw Mau Mau as an enemy just as Britain had done. While Mau Mau would have been an enemy of the elite which took over power to serve their own interests, it was no enemy of the people of Kenya whose demands during the War of Independence was land and freedom as part of independence. As Tandon 2017b says, "Political independence is a significant stage in the fight against imperialism. The 'common man' is brought into the democratic process directly". There can then be no doubt that independence was the first step in the total liberation from imperialism which Kenyan people have been struggling against for generations.

There is, however, a legitimate question to be answered as to whether Mau Mau can be referred to as a revolution or whether it was just a revolt or a resistance. It certainly was not a revolution in the sense of the Russian or the Chinese Revolutions, which overthrew the old class order and ushered in working class into power. Yet it was revolutionary in the sense that it led to the withdrawal of British colonialism and cleared the way for Kenya's independence. Defeat of colonialism is not seen as revolution, whether in India or countries in Africa. Academics and historians can debate the appropriate words to describe the defeat of colonialism, but the term, as used in this book, has the limited meaning of overthrowing the colonial regime and its replacement by a government of an independent country. It is recognised that there needs to be a struggle for economic liberation from imperialism when working people come to power in a truly revolutionary change. In that sense Mau Mau and the War of Independence were not revolutionary wars. Ndegwa (1977) sees the battle as being lost, but the war was won:

However, although the Freedom Fighters are said to have lost the battle, it could be said that they won the war. Soon after the end of the state of emergency, Kenya's independence was declared in December 1963.

Mau Mau had made the British think again about the people they had colonized. It had made them realize that the local people were a force to reckon with. It was not surprising that the British were ready to see the Kenyan people in a different light; they were no longer the meek, obedient and good natives they had always been, but people who knew what they wanted and had ideas of how to get it.

Much was achieved by the struggle, however one describes it. Independence would not have been possible in 1963 without the input from Mau Mau. In addition, Kaggia, B., Leeuw and Kaggia, M (2012) set out other achievements of Mau Mau succinctly:

Mau Mau was an organization formed to achieve what KAU had failed to achieve through constitutional means. It was ready to achieve its objective by any means. It was a movement determined to achieve Kenya's real liberation at any cost. As to what Mau Mau achieved, only blind people could fail to appreciate the many concessions which the British Government granted Kenya. These concessions were what KAU had been demanding for years. During the early months of the Emergency the Colonial Secretary said no change would be possible until the revolt was squashed, and before the beginning of the armed struggle, there was no sign of any change being granted. The British Government followed one concession by another, and it was clear that while the British tried on the one hand to discredit Mau Mau as a primitive organization whose only aim was to return the tribe to the past, at another level the Government accepted the fact that Mau Mau was political and that hostilities would only end with political advancement for Africans.

Even before independence, Mau Mau had changed the political climate in Kenya. Kaggia, B. Leeuw and M. Kaggia (2012) point to some other achievements:

As a result of the Mau Mau armed struggle, the following changes were effected by the British government within a short time. These changes paved the way to independence:

1. In 1954 a new constitution (the Lyttelton plan) started by giving Africans, for the first time in Kenya's history, one minister in the government.

2. In 1955 the Coutts Commission was appointed to work on demarcation of African constituencies and to devise a method of voting for Africans.

3. In the same year the ban on political parties was lifted and Africans were allowed to form district political parties.

4. In 1956 two portfolios were given to Africans.

5. In 1957 limited voting rights were given to Africans and the number of African members of Parliament increased to 8.

6. In 1958 the number of African members of Parliament increased to 14.

7. In 1959 Emergency Governor, Sir Evelyn Baring, was removed from office. He had vowed for years to crash Mau Mau.

8. Britain agreed to a round table conference with the African members to decide on Kenya's future.

Venys (1970) sums up the overall achievements of Mau Mau:

It was the first conscious attempt at an armed anti-colonial revolt in Africa which had no analogy on the continent at that time... The Mau Mau movement has held a unique position in the modern history of Africa as it was the first anti-colonial movement of its kind that produced an armed uprising and persisted for such a long time against the superior force of the colonial power. It was the first manifestation of the strength of subjugated Africans and became a turning point in Kenya's struggle for uhuru ... the movement influenced the subsequent political development of Kenya. It helped the African masses involved in the movement get out of political passivity, providing them with a chance to experience the first lesson in the fight against colonialism. It forced the colonial government [to admit] that the times when the African could be considered nothing but a "poor uncivilised thing" had passed and that there were enormous potentiality hidden in Kenya Africans. The colonialists came to realise that the time had come when Africans must be allowed to participate in the ruling of the country and eventually to run it by themselves. The insurrection was a serious warning indicating that there was something corrupt in the Colony of Kenya and that colonialism in its old shape had ceased to function.

It was Uganda's then Prime Minister Milton Obote who summed up the achievement of Mau Mau in a speech when Kenya achieved independence:

> Today is the day on which Kenya formally joins Algeria at the high rank of being the hero of colonial Africa. The struggle in Kenya was bitter. Many people lost their lives ... The past cannot be forgotten ... It cannot be forgotten because it is the past not only of Kenya but of world history.
> [37]

And it cannot be forgotten because the aims for which many lives were lost are as valid today as they were then. Nor can the example of the brave warriors be forgotten, warriors who, as one of the Mau Mau struggle song records, declared:

> "It is better to die on our feet
> Than to live on our knees".

Kaggia, B., Leeum and Kaggia, M (2012) provide a fitting tribute to Mau Mau:

> The Mau Mau struggle, whether one likes it or not, will stand in history as one of the greatest liberation struggles in Africa. It was the first of its kind on the continent. Its heroes will be remembered by generations to come ... The greatness of the Mau Mau struggle becomes more striking when one remembers that the fighters had no outside contacts, arms supplies or money. Mau Mau relied on its own resources. Money was collected from followers and supporters. In addition to capturing arms, the soldiers manufactured their own. It is time to recognize their achievements. Long

---

[37]   Daily Nation (Nairobi) December 13, 1963.

live Mau Mau! Long live the freedom of Kenya, which the Mau Mau fought for and brought about.

Mathu (1974) looked back at the movement some years after hostilities ceased and sounds a warning about lack of change:

> Looking back on "Mau Mau" today, I still consider it to have been a just and courageous struggle for freedom. Though mistakes were made and some people entered the revolt for narrow or selfish interests, the Kikuyu people as a whole fought and suffered bravely and I am proud of them. Our fight against British colonialism, by throwing fear into the hearts of the imperialists and Settlers, quickened the pace of political development and independence in Kenya. I should like to remind those African leaders who now condemn Mau Mau and tell us to forget our past struggles and suffering, that their present positions of power in the Legislative Council and elsewhere would not have been realized except for our sacrifices. I would also warn them that we did not make these sacrifices just to have Africans step into the shoes of our former European masters.

Mathu thus points to the unfinished work of the War of Independence: "Are the masses of people simply to become the slaves of a handful of wealthy Black men?" Pio Gama Pinto's (1963a) suggestion now needs to be taken up seriously:

> The sacrifices of the hundreds of thousands of Kenya's freedom fighters must be honoured by the effective implementation of the policy - a democratic, African, socialist state in which the people have the right to be free from economic exploitation and the right to social equality. Kenya's *uhuru* [independence] must not be transformed into freedom to exploit, or freedom to be hungry and live in ignorance. *Uhuru* must be uhuru for the masses - *uhuru* from exploitation, from ignorance, disease and poverty.

Mukami Kimathi, Dedan Kimathi's wife and a Mau Mau warrior in her own right, also a detainee at Kamiti Prison where her husband was killed, assessed Mau Mau and called for restoration of justice (Venys, 1970):

> Dedan Kimathi's wife took the platform (on the day of *Uhuru* celebration, December 12, 1963) and declared emphatically that the bloodshed by

Mau Mau in the forest had brought Kenya's independence and all land confiscated by the colonial government from former Mau Mau fighters should be returned to them.

Barnett and Njama (1966) sum up the transition to neo-colonialism:

The revolt of the Kikuyu peasantry lasted for more than three years. Though defeated militarily, few objective observers would deny that there was more than mere coincidence in the fact that the official end of the State of Emergency in January 1960 occurred while British colonial officials at the Lancaster House Conference were agreeing to an African majority in the Kenya Legislative Council and eventual independence for Kenya under African rule. The lowering of the Union Jack in Kenya on 12 December 1963 was unquestionably the culmination of political forces set in motion by the 1953-56 peasant revolution called 'Mau Mau'.

Furedi (1989) provides an overview of the significance of Mau Mau within an African context:

The weakness of political coherence should not obscure the important achievements of the Mau Mau leadership. In contrast to general experience in colonial Africa the mass movement emerged with its own plebeian leadership. This represented a major innovation in the history of Kenyan nationalism. With Mau Mau, for the first time the mass movement acted independently of the educated middle-class leadership. Consequently, here was a mass movement not susceptible to co-optation. The colonial administration had no choice but to destroy it. The growth of Mau Mau can be seen not merely as the result of the strength of the mass movement but also as a symptom of the weakness of the middle-class moderate nationalists. A central theme of colonial policy in the subsequent period was to make sure that this would never happen in the future.

The stage was set for the next phase of resistance to neo-colonialism and imperialism.

Advice for Someone Going into Prison

You must insist on living,
There may not be happiness
but it is your binding duty
to resist the enemy,
and live one extra day.

Inside, ten years, or fifteen years
Or even more can be got through
they really can:
Enough that you never let the precious stone
under your left breast grow dull.

- Nazim Hikmet (1949)[38]

Possible Shape of a Mau Mau Government

There can be no doubt that without colonial interference in the process of transition to independence, a government led or influenced by Mau Mau would have come to power. Given that peasants were an important part of Mau Mau, the first acts of such a truly independent government would have been to redress the land issue which was one of the main aims of the War of Independence. This is also the view of Kabubi (2002), a Mau Mau warrior active on the battlefield, when she replied to the question, "What kind of Kenya would have come if Mau Mau had succeeded?":

> I think land distribution would have been given priority. The government posts would have been filled by the patriots who fought for independence, not by loyalists who collaborated with the British".

If peasants and land were one essential foundation of Mau Mau, "Freedom" was the other one. This included political, social and economic freedom from colonial and imperialist interference. Given that trade unions and working classes played a key role in the War of Independence as a whole and in Mau Mau in particular, it takes no leap of imagination to conclude that a Mau Mau-led government would have strengthened workers' rights and circumscribed

---

38 Nazim Hikmet, A Sad State of Freedom. Translated from the Turkish by Taner Baybars and Richard McKane.1990. Warwick: The Grenville Press.

those of transnational corporations and reduced or eliminated the influence of foreign governments in deciding government policies. Social and political rights of nationalities, women, working people generally would have been protected.

However an objective assessment of Mau Mau needs to examine what Mau Mau did not achieve. It did not achieve the two aims of "land and freedom". Here the freedom is defined not in terms of independence only but in the broader sense of power and control over policies that would change the life chances of working people. The return of the stolen land to their rightful owners was a key demand of the War of Independence. It was removed from national agenda by the independence government with the connivance of the colonial government. Added to this is the scuppering of the agenda set out by the trade union movement under the East African Trade Union Congress (EATUC). The colonial government and the comprador government sidelined the demands of EATUC by restricting trade union rights and curtailing the political aspects of trade union activities while co-opting the trade union movement as part of the comprador government.

The question then arises whether there was anything that Mau Mau could have done to ensure success in meeting its broader objective. Maloba (1998) mentions that Mau Mau lacked a strong political party which could have completed the work that political and military activists had carried out in the country. While there was a political structure that was beginning to emerge with the Kenya Parliament, this process had not reached fruition by the time the British colonial government decided that independence with moderate elements it had nurtured was a better option than delayed independence, which would allow the full force of Mau Mau's revolutionary programme to develop. This was one of the reasons for the rush to independence that was instigated by the last Governor of Kenya, Sir Malcolm McDonald. Just as at an earlier stage, British colonialism had prevented the full preparation of the military development of Mau Mau, in the late 1950s and early 1960s, it similarly scuppered the normal political development that could possibly have seen the emergence of a Mau Mau political Party with aims as set out by Pinto (1963a) above. In the absence of such a militant party, the way was clear for conservative politicians nurtured by colonialism to become the rulers to replace colonialism. The marginalisation of Mau Mau in these two aspects - the military and political - can be seen as the long term victory of imperialism over the people of Kenya.

And yet it would be unfair to judge Mau Mau on the basis that it did not achieve the results whose time had not come during their period. The contradiction of the time was with European Settlers and colonial government and that was certainly settled in favour of Mau Mau as the British military and political manoeuvring could not delay independence. The battle against neo-colonialism could not be waged in the period of colonialism. It is to the credit of Mau Mau that it highlighted and started preparing for the fight against the new face of imperialism even as it was succeeding in its anti-colonial battles. Its military preparedness, ideological struggles and communications strategy were once again gearing up for the new struggles ahead. And the long-term war against imperialism was set to continue after independence, this time by successors of Mau Mau.

Reparation

British colonialism has ended. It has left major problems for Kenya in a similar way it did in India, as Tharoor (2016c) says:

> British rule de-industrialised India, created landlessness and poverty, drained our country's resources, exploited, enslaved, exiled and oppressed millions, sowed seeds of division and inter-communal hatred that led to the country's partitioning into two hostile states, and was directly responsible for the deaths of 35 million people in unnecessary and mismanaged famines as well as of thousands in massacres and killings. That just skims the surface of the havoc wreaked by British colonialism. The British conquered one of the richest countries in the world and reduced it to one of the poorest.

So is it time to think of reparations that Britain needs to make to people of Kenya - and India and other former colonies - for the damage it has done? Tharoor (2016c) does not think so, but it seems only for technical reasons:

> But I don't in fact ask for reparations, as the Oxford debate did. How do you place a monetary value on all that India suffered and lost under British rule? There's really no compensation that would even begin to be adequate, or credible. The symbolic pound-a-year I'd suggested would

be a nightmare to administer.

And there are other difficulties in getting reparation. Quantifying damage in a situation that is highlighted by Bufacchi (2017) can be a daunting task:

> Any debate about the best way to rectify historical injustice must take into account the violence at the heart of the injustice, its arbitrariness, and enduring qualities ... in the context of colonialism the violence is fundamentally different from the violence that one finds in a democracy. The difference is the arbitrary nature of colonial violence, and arbitrariness is what makes colonialism not just wrong but distinctively so.

Similarly, Tharoor (2016a) raises another legacy of colonialism that is difficult to address in the neo-colonial phase:

> Empire might have gone, but it endures in the imitative elites it left behind in the developing world, the 'mimic men', in Naipaul's phrase, trying hard to be what the imperial power had not allowed them to be, while subjecting themselves and their societies to the persistent domination of corporations based mainly in the metropole. The East India Company has collapsed but globalization has ensured that its modern-day successors in the former imperial states remain the predominant instruments of capitalism.

And yet colonialism cannot be allowed to cause permanent damage to the former colonised peoples and not pay for its crimes. We need to separate the technical and other difficulties in getting reparation from the moral case for making reparations. And it should not be a few individuals who can decide if and how reparations need to be made. It is for the people of former colonies to decide in partnership with the people of the countries that colonised them - certainly not the elite and not the corporations in both the countries which benefited from decades of exploitation and repression. History is on their side.

Neo-colonialism, the Legacy of Colonialism

The War of Independence was waged against the system of exploitation. This system itself had undergone changes in response to the military attacks of Mau Mau. By about 1956-57, it became clear that colonialism was no longer sustainable in Kenya. The departure of British colonialism was a matter of time. In just a few years of warfare, Mau Mau had changed the balance of power, although it had to pay a heavy price for this change, with many combatants injured, dead, in detention or maimed. Many others had lost their land, livestock and means of livelihood, their children having to grow up without adequate food, clothing, housing or education. The new independent Government of Kenya cast them aside even as the new power holders, who had played an insignificant or no part in the struggle for independence, became the new rich class with the power, wealth, land, jobs and education denied to Mau Mau activists and their children. But Mau Mau militants had realised quite early the danger of colonialist tentacles returning to take control of the country in a new form. They clearly saw colonialists "going from the door, only to return through the window" as neo-colonialists.

From that initial realisation of the new threat to the young Kenyan nation right up to and beyond the time of formal independence in 1963, all the energies of Mau Mau cadres was poured into making people aware of the new danger facing the revolution. Ideological and military preparations had to be made for another struggle before final victory could be achieved.

These renewed Mau Mau preparations were admitted by the colonial regime in the last years of its existence. Thus the colonial minister of Internal Security and Defence (the ministry charged with fighting Mau Mau), Mr Swann, had to admit that "for the last three months of 1962, operations have progressed to curb the activities of the Kenya Land and Freedom Army." He revealed that the colonial government was detaining more people "to avoid a second emergency in Kenya". Mr Swann said that the purpose of Mau Mau was to take over power in Kenya. "An emergency would be inevitable if we had not taken any action this year", he added.

Mr Swann admitted that in spite of the vast military intervention of top military forces in Kenya since 1952 and even earlier "he did not hope to stamp out the type of activity typified by Mau Mau and the Kenya Land and Freedom Army ... this activity will never stop". He made a number of observations in this period which shows that Mau Mau continued its organisational and military activities in this new period of neo-colonialism. Below are some of his comments, and reports from newspapers of the time taken from Kenya Committee's Press Extracts:

> It was hoped to secure the help of Jomo Kenyatta after his release. "We have discussed the Kenya Land and Freedom Army with Kenyatta and he is certainly not in favour of it", Mr. Swann said. "I hope to enlist him as well as other leaders".
>
> ...
>
> The reorganized Kenya Land and Freedom Army consisted of a Committee representing various parts of Kenya, and it (was) the Supreme Command ... It revived also among Mau Mau detainees in Mbagathi prison in 1957. They started work on the organization.
>
> ...
>
> The Kenya Land and Freedom Army was still organizing, and had launched a recruiting campaign. Its cry was not for action now but in the future. It could be planned for the end of the year, for internal self-government, or for independence. The idea is to secure more members and more weapons now.
>
> ...
>
> The pattern of oathing was the same - to preserve secrecy, maintain unity, never cooperate with the [colonial] government ... steal arms and ammunition and money ... commit murder when ordered and to obtain land. (Mathu, 1974).

Mau Mau was preparing, thus the renewed organisational structures, revised ideologies and new military tactics in the period before 1963. Perhaps the most important work in the early years was to warn the people against the new danger. The neo-colonialist allies were constantly pouring forth lies and falsehoods through their mass media with their message that independence was just round the corner, hence there was no need to struggle any more. The goals of the struggle for independence were won, they said; Africanisation and multiracialism were here, they proclaimed, so there was no longer a need to continue the fight.

It thus became necessary to bring the ideological battle to the forefront. It became necessary to place before the people a correct analysis of historical events, and to emphasise the need to continue the struggle. This was done in the form of a Policy Document which was widely circulated. It was also presented at the Conference of the Kenya African National Union held in Nairobi in December 1961, where contradictions were developing about the need to combat neo-colonialism. The Document, entitled "The Struggle for Kenya's Future" was the clearest statement on the dangers of neo-colonialism. It is reproduced in Appendix B.

Some aspects of this struggle for the future of Kenya are examined in the rest of the book.

A Prison Without Walls[39]

There are no walls
In this prison
It is built on a foundation of fear, intimidation, and threats.

Keep the history book closed, keep the historian in prison

The prison without walls
Has room for many.

How to subdue
The anger of millions
Who see their sweat and blood enriching but a few?

Concentration camps and stone prisons are never enough.
Gallows will not silence them
They are too many, far too many.

Quick, open the gates
Gates of the prison without walls. Create a terror
Worse than death.

---

39 Written by the author in London on October 20, 1984 to mark Mau Mau Freedom Fighters' Day.

No evidence of violence
No, not even a scratched forehead. Yet opposition is silenced
Millions are struck dumb.

Blame the victim
Make the innocent guilty for questioning their misery, for being.

Interrogations, threats, and insults.
Why think? Why not be an animal? Threaten by suggestions, intimidate by
looks

Will your child be safe?

The prison without walls
Is never full
Bring in more and still more
Until the whole country becomes
A prison house without a single wall.

And yet
Questions keep coming
Voices of protest keep singing, minds keep working, day and night, day and
night

The prison without walls
Will never solve the problem. Only the united will
Of the people will.

Kenya became independent on December 12, 1963. Now an African Prime
Minister and an African government ruled the country. The old order had
given way to the new. And that achievement was due entirely to Mau Mau.

And yet it was not the independence that those who participated in the War
of Independence had fought for. The changes were soon seen for what they
were: the replacement of colonialism by neo-colonialism, the replacement of
European Settlers by African "owners" of land. European Settlers remained,
as did multinational corporations as the rulers behind the scene. Government

policies were handed down by the "independent" government in Nairobi but directed by imperialist forces in London and New York. Policy guidance came from IMF and the World Bank. The only aspect that did not change was the condition of working class, the situation of those who fought in the war of independence. It was, in effect, independence of the ruling classes (black and white this time) to rule, kill, massacre, suppress and loot as they pleased. And suppress, kill and massacre they needed to in order to remain in power as the people who had sacrificed all were not yet ready to hand over control to new masters with the same agenda. But the new masters were fully backed by the same imperialist powers which had engineered their coming to power.

Field Marshal Muthoni (2007) has no hesitation in identifying this neo-colonialist hijacking of Kenya's independence:

> It's like a competitive match. We were the team. We played valiantly, sacrificially, against the opposing team. We sweated. We gave our lives. Then, at the end of the match, when we had won, the spectators ran away with the trophy.

Field Marshal Muthoni (2007) explains what happened at the time of independence with clarity and understanding:

> Come independence, 1963 is when the injustice of the system began to set in. Mau Mau readily gave up their weapons and returned to their villages. The struggle, after all, had been won. Reality proved somewhat less than ideal. They found that, while they were in the forest fighting the enemy, land consolidation had taken place in 1960. Those who were absent had had their land taken away from them and given to others. They found that, while they were fighting, those they had left in the villages had been educating themselves and educating their children. The fledgling government needed this educated cadre as it began to establish itself. So therefore, it was the children of those who did not fight who were offered positions of influence in government on account of their experience and education.

And these things happened not as an accident but as a result of a carefully planned exit of colonialism which eased the way for the smooth entry of neo-colonialism. Mau Mau achieved one of the key aims of the War of Independence which was to defeat colonialism and achieve independence for Kenya. In this, it also changed British colonial policy and perhaps hastened the independence of other African countries. Yet gaining political independence was not the only aim of the War of Independence as the document, *The Struggle For Kenya's Future (1972)*,[40] made clear:

> The struggle for Kenya's future is being waged today on three distinct though interrelated levels - political, racial and economic. It seems to us that we Africans are being allowed to "win" in the first two spheres as long as we don't contest the battle being waged on the third, all-important economic level.

An indication of things to come after independence was given by Jomo Kenyatta, as Venys (1970) records:

> Within six months of *Uhuru*, Kenyatta was publicly denouncing activities of the rebels. He found it necessary to travel in the affected areas warning people against oath-taking and supporting the forest rebels to whom he referred as "vagabonds". Kenyatta continued the policies of the now departed colonialists and had General Baimungi, General Chui and other Mau Mau leaders assassinated in 1965. He described Mau Mau as "…a disease which has been eradicated and must never be remembered again" (*East African Standard, September 10, 1962*).

The fear that the imperialist enemy would exit through the door only to return through the window came to pass in the form of an "enemy within". Kenya provides a good example of what Thomsen (2017) refers to as "the attempt of imperialism to turn back the wheel of history to colonial times". While this may not have happened in all its details, the oppression of working class was certainly reimposed. Given that the oppression and exploitation continued after independence, the War of Independence entered its second phase with the attainment of independence.

But the situation that Kenyans found themselves in was not unique as imperialism was well prepared to combat people's resistance. Thus it was not

---

40   Reproduced in Appendix B.

only in Kenya that imperialism eliminated resistance leaders and planted seeds of division among people. The experience of South Africa at a later time was similar to what happened in Kenya, as Kasrils (2013) recalls:

> South Africa's liberation struggle reached a high point but not its zenith when we overcame apartheid rule. Back then, our hopes were high for our country given its modern industrial economy, strategic mineral resources (not only gold and diamonds), and a working class and organised trade union movement with a rich tradition of struggle. But that optimism overlooked the tenacity of the international capitalist system. From 1991 to 1996 the battle for the ANC's soul got under way, and was eventually lost to corporate power: we were entrapped by the neoliberal economy – or, as some today cry out, we "sold our people down the river".

But the subversion of African liberation and the elimination of leaders who stood against imperialism also indicates that there was a systematic plan to eliminate all progressive movements and leaders, as the article, *Every Leader Who Stood Up...* (2017) in *How Africa News* records:

> One by one, our most steadfast leaders have been eliminated, to the point where Africa is hard-pressed to point out more than three people who are advancing the continental agenda for economic freedom. Almost every single leader who has stood up for Africa's right to economic self-determination has been eliminated – either physically or politically.

The process did not start in the 20th Century, nor with the elimination of Kwame Nkrumah in Ghana and Patrice Lumumba in the Congo. It started right at the beginning of colonialism itself and continued with the elimination of Dedan Kimathi and systematic attacks on Mau Mau. And it continues unabated today.

The response in Kenya, as elsewhere in Africa, is the continuation of the struggle for total liberation, particularly in the economic field. The War of Economic Independence is continued by the political successors of Mau Mau.

114

Sina Habari, Mwanangu: I have No News, My Child[41]

I have no news, my child
no news at all
Except
news of troubles, torture and death.

I have no news, people of my land
no news at all
If you want land, food, shelter, clothing
no news at all
Except
News of bullets and wars.

I have no news, patriot
no news at all
If you want freedom, liberation, liberty
I have no news
Except
News of struggle and struggles

Colonialism's Secret Weapon

In the long run, the tactic that appears to have ended Mau Mau's armed resistance was the British Government's use of Homeguard force to divide Kenyan people and to infiltrate ranks of resistance. In what was to develop in later years as contra-forces and similar local mercenary forces under US imperialism, British colonialism used an early version of the same disruptive force. Anderson (2016) shows that this use was not confined to Kenya:

> In all the wars of decolonization fought across Africa and Asia from the 1940s until the 1970s, European colonial powers deployed local forces to battle against armed nationalist groups. These local allied combatants, variously known as auxiliaries, militias or loyalists when drawn together in irregular forces, or sometimes more formally recruited to swell the ranks of police or military reserves, often became a critically important component of colonial counter-insurgencies.

---

41   Translation of Sina Habari, Mwanangu (Kiswahili) by Shiraz Durrani (1985).

While such loyalist forces were used against the armed combatants of Mau Mau, they were also used as a weapon to overcome the militancy of Kenyan War of Independence at economic and political levels. The use of divisive politics by Britain continued as they sought to ensure a situation favourable to imperialism, as Wasserman (1976) explains:

> When the fighting war came to an end, loyalist leaders were therefore consolidated as a ruling elite in Central Province, given control of administrative positions as local government was restored from 1956, and then shepherded into government as Kenya's decolonization got underway from 1959. Their monopoly of local politics was secured by laws that prevented known rebels from participating in elections, and once in positions of authority they were able to exclude former Mau Mau from many areas of public life, while also blocking any attempt they made to restore their lost property or to recover their forfeited land.

> Kikuyu loyalists were the building blocks with which Kenya's post-colonial state was constructed in Central Province, and in the 1960s they even came to dominate the political economy of the entire country.

A Brief Recap

A brief recap of what Britain did in Kenya would help set the background to understanding the impact colonialism had on people and the country and what imperialism sets out to do after independence. Leigh Day (2016) summarises British brutality:

> On 24 April 1954, the Colonial Administration launched an assault on the Mau Mau which was known as "Operation Anvil", whereby 17,000 Mau Mau suspects were rounded up and incarcerated in detention camps without trial. Detainees were moved from one camp to another, where the treatment was of increasing or decreasing severity depending on the detainee's willingness to cooperate and denounce the Mau Mau. In particular, detainees were expected to confess that they had taken "the Mau Mau oath" and to repent of having done so.

> In 1954, a process known as "villagisation" was initiated and with

approximately 1 million Kenyans were forced to burn their homes and rounded up for six years in 854 villages fenced with barbed wire where acts of brutality by colonial guards were widespread.

It is estimated by historians that, over the years which followed, as many as 150,000 suspected Mau Mau members and sympathisers were detained without trial in a labyrinth of about 150 detention camps and 'screening centres' littered around Kenya known as 'the Pipeline'.

From the inception of the detention camps, the Colonial Administration engaged in widespread acts of brutality. Detainees were subjected to arbitrary killings, severe physical assaults and extreme acts of inhuman and degrading treatment.

The acts of torture included castration and sexual assaults which, in many cases, entailed the insertion of broken bottles into the vaginas of female detainees.

Camp guards engaged in regular severe beatings and assaults, often resulting in death. In the course of interrogations in some cases guards would hang detainees upside down and insert sand and water into their anuses.

> In 1957, the Colonial Administration decided to subject the detainees who still refused to cooperate and comply with orders to a torture technique known as 'the dilution technique'. The technique involved the systematic use of brute force to overpower the Mau Mau adherents, using fists, clubs, truncheons and whips.

> This brutality would continue until the detainees cooperated with orders and ultimately confessed and repented of their alleged Mau Mau allegiance.

Leigh Day (2016) goes on to quote Professor Elkins who adds to this grim picture:

> There is no record of how many people died as a result of torture, hard labour, sexual abuse, malnutrition, and starvation. We can make an informed evaluation of the official statistic of eleven thousand Mau Mau

killed by reviewing the historical evidence we know ... The impact of the detention camps and villages goes well beyond statistics. Hundreds of thousands of men and women have quietly lived with the damage - physical, psychological, and economic - that was inflicted upon them during the Mau Mau war.

And it is even worse than this. The seeds of destruction of a peaceful development of Kenya were planted right at the beginning of British colonialism. It is necessary for those who resist imperialism today to be equipped with appropriate information about how their country was sold out to imperialism by colonialism and its chosen Kenyan elite. The following brief section documents this process which needs more additional research and analysis.

Neo-colonialism Entrenched

As far as the British Establishment is concerned, Mau Mau is a closed chapter, the War of Independence did not take place, Kenya was "given" independence by Britain. And so imperialism can carry on its work, freed from colonial baggage. But the adverse effects of the colonial manipulation on the working people of the former colonies continue to this day. It actively planned Kenya's future so that the colonial aims were achieved under imperialism, which is now led by USA. African elite now are the local delivery boys and girls of the imperialist enterprise.

From the time that it was realised, around 1959, that the War of Independence under Mau Mau leadership would force colonialism out of Kenya and that independence was inevitable, colonialists actively organised a "friendly coup" to enable takeover of power by an elite favourably inclined towards the new imperialist alliance, USA and Britain. The political position was to ensure that moderate leaders groomed by colonialism came to power at independence and to marginalise and eliminate (physically in some cases) those who supported or represented Mau Mau's radical programme for land and freedom. That this was well planned and delivered by the British Government is obvious as the following section from an early draft of Durrani, Shiraz (forthcoming) indicates:

But the radical wing of KANU in the years before independence and its subsequent development into the Kenya People's Union under Oginga

Odinga faced not only internal but external enemies too. The departing colonial power, Britain, now joined by the new imperialist superpower, USA, had already decided to ensure that independent Kenya would be run by the moderates. They fully supported the Kenyatta moderate wing as a way of stopping the radicals who, in effect, were carrying on the revolutionary agenda of Mau Mau. While the elimination of the radical wing was supposedly done by the Kenyatta moderates, the power behind their actions was the colonial government which cleverly dispatched a so-called progressive to be the Governor of Kenya to oversee the transition of the colony to a Western neo-colony under the guise of independence. The last Governor of Kenya, Malcolm MacDonald (MacDonald, 1976b) - self proclaimed Moderate Socialist - explains the thinking of the colonial government regarding the moderate-radical contradiction in Kenya in response to the question, "I remember you saying earlier that it was wise for the British Government to support Kenyatta because he was a moderate":

I thought that if the moderates ... came into power in independent Kenya they would not only be moderate in their national policies, in economic and social and political affairs, but on the side of moderation in international affairs, and for example not go communist and not come under the influence of any other communist anti-British anti-Western power.

The significance of this support of colonial power goes beyond the control over Kenyan politics after independence. It helped to overturn the entire Mau Mau programme of change and their quest for land, freedom and justice. The radicals were well aware of this neo-colonial danger as they pointed out in 1961 in their document The *Struggle for Kenya's Future*, quoted earlier. The British support for the moderates was crucial in ensuring that a regime compliant with Western interests came to power and remains in power to date. This support for the moderates included the suppression of progressive trade unions, political parties and social movements as well as marginalisation and undermining of radical leaders.

And the last British Governor in Kenya and the British Government met their objectives of selecting Jomo Kenyatta as the first Prime Minister of Kenya. The subsequent land grabbing by the successive KANU regimes of Kenyatta and Moi has been confirmed in recently available documents of the last Colonial Governor of Kenya, Sir Malcolm MacDonald and those of the former Vice President of Kenya, Joseph Murumbi. Ng'otho (2008) reveals the land issue from both these sources:

> Fresh evidence pieced together by the Sunday Nation confirms widespread speculation that Kenya's first president Jomo Kenyatta entered a secret pact with the British government not to interfere with the skewed land distribution at independence. In return, the British would clear his way as independent Kenya's first leader which looked impossible only three years to freedom. Kenyatta would later extract a similar pledge from his successor, retired president Daniel arap Moi.

And Kenyatta duly fulfilled his side of the colonial bargain with his colonial masters, as the Truth, Justice and Reconciliation Commission (TJRC,2013) records:

> In his independence speech, Jomo Kenyatta did not suggest any substantial change in the colonial structures. The colonial state would remain intact – despite the fact that the fight for national independence had been dominated by demands for social justice, egalitarian reforms, participatory democracy, prosecution of those who had committed mass killings and other forms of crimes during the ar of Independence, and the abolition of the colonial state and its oppressive institutions ... Also, in his independence speech, Jomo Kenyatta never mentioned the heroism of the Mau Mau movement. No Mau Mau freedom songs were sung, no KLFA leaders were allowed to speak during the historic day. Instead, Kenyatta asked the people to forget the past – to forgive and forget the atrocities committed against them by the British and their Kenyan supporters during the war of independence.

That sums up the imperialist plot against the people of Kenya, with the connivance of the elite groomed by colonialism. Wasserman (1976) completes the story:

> Mau Mau remained banned until 2003. Public silence about Mau Mau

was a means to avoid discussion of the unfinished business of the Emergency, and a way to prevent claims being made against loyalists. The loyalist bargain therefore consolidated the authority of the independent Kenyan state, first shaping the settlement that was made in the process of decolonization, and then securing the position of the political elite who governed the country. And impunity was not an idea confined to colonial Kenya. In 1970, Kenyatta's loyalist Attorney General, Charles Njonjo, would pass into law the Indemnity Act, to 'protect the activities of government officials and security officers.' This was specifically aimed at thwarting the prosecution of soldiers and police for acts of atrocity committed in northern Kenya, between 1962 and 1967, during the Shifta War against Somali insurgents. Until its annulment in 2010, this act came to represent 'the institutionalisation of impunity in Kenya.'

Thus colonialism handed over to the independent government of Kenya some of the most poisonous weapons that were directed against people demanding what Mau Mau had always demanded.

Oppression and Exploitation: Gifts of the British Empire

The British colonial government's legacy of impunity as it massacred, murdered and tortured people at will was then bequeathed to the governments it set up after independence. The lesson that colonialism passed on to the comprador regime would seem to be that it is acceptable to eliminate and destroy people who oppose their policies and government for the elite and imperialism. Pio Gama Pinto was the first martyr in a long line of leaders eliminated. And individuals were not the only targets: entire communities and populations were "cleansed" and made refugees when they refused to support the elite rulers. And massacres and genocide were also part of this imperialist arsenal. The armed forces, officially serving the people, became their oppressors and a weapon of the elite against the people. The TJRC (2013, Vo.IIA, 72) records the events of the time:

> Kenyatta, having realized that he would not be able to meet the needs and expectations of all Kenyans, engaged in measures that would ensure political survival and self sustenance of his government. This lead to a strengthening of the role of the security agencies similar to the role they

played during the colonial period, and particularly aimed at controlling, and suppressing dissent and organized political opposition. In brief, in the words of Charles Hornsby, 'the Independent State soon echoed its colonial parents repressive attitudes to dissent'.

The three governments after independence continued to use as a normal practice political assassinations of those they perceived as enemies as a normal practice. With the support of police and army at a national level and implicit agreement of USA and UK governments at international level, the use of such assassinations became a normal way of dealing with political issues. TJRC Report (2013) says:

> Political assassinations have occurred under each of the three successive governments since independence. The motives associated with these assassinations have varied, from getting rid of political competition, weeding out ambitious politicians, and removing perceived "dissidents" of the government or those who posed as "threats" to power. Evidence of state involvement and subsequent cover-ups is evident in the majority of political murders. Propaganda and commissions of inquiry are often used as smokescreens to get to "the bottom of the matter," and often have the effect of masking the motives and faces behind the assassinations. Prominent figures in government are said to be implicated. Key witnesses into the assassinations disappear or die mysteriously. No real perpetrators have ever been prosecuted, much less effectively investigated. (TJRC Final Report, Vol.IIA).

The Truth, Justice and Reconciliation Commission (TJRC, 1913) documented extra-judicial killings stretching back to the colonial period, when an estimated 90,000 people were executed, tortured or injured during the crackdown against the Mau Mau uprising. During those operations, over 160,000 people were detained in appalling conditions.

Upon attaining independence, the country witnessed political assassinations during President Jomo Kenyatta's tenure, says, TJRC Report, "Kenyatta was president during the deaths of Field Marshall Baimungi (1964), Pio Gama Pinto (1965), Kungu Karumba (who disappeared since June 14 1974), Tom Mboya (July 5 1975), Ronald Ngala (12 December 1972), J.M Kariuki (March 2 1975) and Argwings Kodhek (1969) ... The investigations into these deaths were quite cursory. The lack of serious investigation into these killings created the public perception that the truth about these killings was yet to be established".

During the post-Jomo Kenyatta era, the political assassinations continued, according to TJRC. "Extra-judicial killings during this time also took place in the form of shooting and killing of political dissidents, as well as deaths during detention," says the commission. The commission cited instances where people were killed for questioning extra-judicial killings by police.

Repression by the regime ensured that there was no public outcry against such official action. The support of USA and Britain ensured that the regime was let off the hook internationally too. But the seeds of massacres and murders had been sown by the departing colonial regime and the favoured leaders after independence used the same colonial methods to stay in power.

Durrani, Shiraz (forthcoming) looks at the machinations behind the scenes that Britain used to ensure their favoured politicians came to power after independence:

> By bringing in the Cold War logic into the Kenyan situation, the Governor [Malcolm MacDonald] and the British Government succeeded in ensuring the moderates they could trust and work with became the new Government of independent Kenya. But this was no last minute planning. MacDonald, upon arriving in Kenya 1962, decided to speed up the process of independence planned by London for late 1964 or early 1965. His reasons for early independence in 1963 makes interesting reading as they relate to ensuring that the moderates came to power at independence. MacDonald (1976a) says:

> The reason why I thought the transition should be speeded up was that the "moderates" were in control of both KANU and KADU. Jomo Kenyatta was not supposed to be a "moderate", but I decided within a few days that he was one... I felt that if independence didn't come as quickly as they wanted, they would lose influence with a lot of their supporters, and the more extreme, less reasonable and capable politicians would take over. I thought it would be a great mistake to allow that to happen.

This manipulation of Kenyan political process is what led to the philosophy of Mau Mau, progressed by the militant wing of KANU, losing out to the moderates who went on to be one of the most corrupt governments in Africa.

The tactics of "disappearing" people continues to date as Gumbihi (2016) reports:

> A report by Human Rights Watch released in July 2016 indicated that 34 people, including two women, were missing. They were arrested in counter-terrorism crackdowns in northern Kenya between 2013 and 2015. "Kenyan authorities have denied knowledge of the missing people, failed to acknowledge credible evidence of abuses during counterterrorism operations, failed to investigate the allegations and in some instances, intimidate and harass those seeking information and accountability," states the report. The organisation also established that bodies of at least 11 people previously arrested by state agents were found in the last two years.

Britain handed over to the comprador rulers of her former colonies around the world the lasting legacy of the British Empire: tools of economic exploitation and political repression, all backed up by armies usually set up and maintained by imperialism.

Stealing Land "legally": Corruption Entrenched

Land always was, and still remains, the biggest grievance that Kenyan people have and it still remains unresolved, thanks to British colonial policies which independent governments have continued to uphold. But the colonial economic aims in Kenya were to ensure that moderate leaders groomed by colonialism came to power at independence and to marginalise and eliminate (physically in some cases) those who supported or represented Mau Mau's radical programme for land and freedom. Land was, and remains, a crucial issue in Kenya. It was the key demand under colonialism and is at the centre of tension today. It is an issue that cannot be ignored or swept under the carpet.

Truth, Justice and Reconciliation Commission Report (TJRC, 2013,Vol. IIB) examined the land situation in the colonial period:

> ... the establishment of the reserves was another tool applied by the

British colonial administration to further alienate local communities' prime land, thereby exposing communities, over time, to land scarcity and landlessness ... The British administration's efforts to alienate land in mainland Kenya accelerated after World War I, when former British soldiers were encouraged to settle and engage in agricultural production activities and for that purpose, they were allowed to acquire land, ostensibly from the Crown, at concessionary rates. Settlement of ex-soldiers was facilitated by the Ex-Soldier Settlement Scheme and backed by the Crown Lands (Discharged Soldiers Settlement) Ordinance of 1921, Kenya having been declared a British colony in 1920. However, only a limited amount of 'Crown Land' was suitable for settler cultivation and this provided impetus for the colonial government to alienate more land from indigenous Africans, in areas that were deemed to be of high agricultural potential by establishing and confining African communities to what were referred to as "native reserves."

The Report goes on to examine the colonial practice of acquiring land through "coercive measures" and "forced evictions" before looking at an important cause of land shortage that has not been given the prominence it deserves. On "land alienation and displacement by multinational corporations" the report says:

Apart from the colonial administration and its white settler demand for land, multinational corporations, many of which had European origin, also contributed to displacement and landlessness of African communities, especially in Kericho and other parts of the Rift Valley. In various parts of Rift Valley, especially in Kericho, such companies acquired large tracts of land that was initially meant for the resettlement of African communities in the area for cultivation of tea.

The Report also shows the extent of such land policies of the British Government, tying down land deals with 999 year-leases:

Companies that were allocated most of the productive land in the Rift Valley in 1923 on lease for 999 years were, notably: James Finlay Company Limited (formerly the African Highlands Produce Company Ltd) and Unilever Kenya Ltd (formerly Brooke Bond). These companies, among others, acquired land at the expense of the local landless Africans in the affected areas.

The Truth, Justice and Reconciliation Commission Report (TJRC, 2013,Vol. IIB) provides evidence of how the British Government used the so-called emergency to intensify its land alienation policy:

> Repressive tendencies of the British, especially forced eviction of Africans from their homelands, coupled with alienation of evictees' land, which was made worse by, among other things, the suffering of Africans in squalid conditions in the overpopulated reserves and restrictions on African commodity production, precipitated an African freedom movement in the nature of a land and freedom army, known as Mau Mau. The Mau Mau, which comprised members of a number of African ethnic communities that had, among other things, been dispossessed of their land, under the leadership of members of the Kikuyu community, launched several violent assaults against officers serving the colonial administration in Kenya and their African collaborators, in a bid to recover their land and regain freedom from oppression. Attacks organized largely in forest areas and staged by the Mau Mau prompted the colonial government to declare a 'State of Emergency' in Kenya in 1952 and that provided the colonial administration another chance to unjustifiably alienate Africans' land.

During the emergency period, persons suspected to be members of the Mau Mau movement were either killed, detained or repatriated from their settlement schemes, including Olenguruone Settlement Scheme in Nakuru, Rift Valley, from which some of the members of the Mau Mau were repatriated to Central Province. Under the guise of the declared State of Emergency, the British colonial administration took draconian measures against Africans, including repatriation from their settlements, arrest and detention of members or sympathizers of the Mau Mau. Land was alienated from those associated with the Mau Mau and allocated to those who were loyal to the administration as a punishment for what it considered as acts of terror against the settler community. Thus the Mau Mau movement attracted further African land alienation by the colonial administration and attendant landlessness and destitution because when

Mau Mau fighters and their collaborators returned from war, they found that their land and other property had been confiscated by British administration loyalists including 'Homeguards' and the provincial administration. It is noted that the Declaration of Emergency also, as a colonial measure, permitted the colonial administration to suspend hearing and determination of land-related suits in African courts through the enactment of the 1957 African Courts (Suspension of Land Suits) Ordinance, which made it impossible for affected Africans to present their claims in court for redress and thus foreclosed their right to justice in respect of land ownership and utilization in the colonial period.

The TJRC Final Report (2013, Vol.IIB) examines land issues in different parts of the country, including the explosive situation at the Coast:

> ... most of the individuals, families and communities at the Coast ended up living as 'squatters' on land that had either been acquired by Arabs or the British such that by the time Kenya attained independence, many at the Coast had no titles to their land.

The Report highlights the fact that the unequal land policy of British colonialism led to inter-ethnic conflicts which have continued in the period after independence as a lasting legacy of colonialism, reinforced by the refusal of Kenyan governments to change these policies. This refusal is, in fact, part of the independence settlement agreed upon by the British government and its favoured "leaders" at independence.

The TJRC Final Report (2013, Vol.IIB) records that the corruption and injustice of the colonial era continued after independence:

> Official corruption in the acquisition, allocation, ownership and disposal of land in Kenyatta's era continued unabated regardless of the existence of applicable laws and policies that were intended to govern dealings in land ... the coastal region has the largest number of landless people and has been severely marginalized in terms of land adjudication, consolidation and registration. Because of the myriad land problems, the majority of people at the Coast remain very poor; it is the region where land acquisition by individuals and other bodies from outside of

the indigenous ethnic communities (considered as upcountry people) has been the largest. It is also the region where land-related injustices appear to have been the gravest and the longest lasting.

In keeping with his promise of following in the footsteps of Kenyatta, Moi continued Kenyatta's policies on repression and maintaining the rule of the elite minority by force of arms, particularly on corruption. The TJRC Final Report (2013, Vol.IIB) notes his continuing corruption on land issues:

> In August 1978, Daniel arap Moi took over as the second President of the Republic of Kenya following the death of Jomo Kenyatta. He promised to follow the footsteps of his predecessor. Moi's '*Fuata Nyayo*' philosophy literally meant that he would follow in the footsteps of his predecessor in critical aspects of policy and governance, including approval of illegal land allocations, and he did, with the exception of minor policy departures, especially in relation to his pro-pastoralist policy and his new focus on the development of arid and semi-arid lands. During his tenure, every category of government-owned land including military establishments, road reserves, public parks, bus parks, public toilets, forests and cemeteries as well as trust lands were illegally acquired in what became publicly known as the widespread phenomenon of land grabbing, mainly by the president himself, his family, officials in his administration, politicians, civil servants, and military officers. In the process, more than 200,000 illegal title deeds were acquired which ought to be revoked.

The effect of these policies was a massive build-up of wealth and power in the hands of a minority which also controlled state power. Class divisions became sharper. The policies of successive Kenyan governments to entrench illegal wealth transfer have ensured that no revocation of illegal title deeds suggested by the Truth, Justice and Reconciliation Commission takes place. Mau Mau's struggle for land and economic freedom continues in the post-independence period.

What Might Have Been: Independence Without Imperialism

British colonialism used extreme measures such as the declaration of the so-called Emergency, the use of military might, the creation of Homeguard comprador class (both in military and political fields), the use of legal and illegal measures of repression - all to defeat the vision that Mau Mau and Kenya's War of Independence had. It ensured that individuals and political organisations supporting the struggle against imperialism were marginalised, banned, destroyed or eliminated. This colonial programme, aimed at Mau Mau, was also used against militant trade unions, progressive educational institutions, political parties, social movements, newspapers and mass media. No individuals, no social force that did not support imperialism was spared. In Mau Mau, it had a particularly difficult opponent who refused to cave in even in the face of the military might of the British Empire and continued its struggle even when colonialism had created a new pro-imperialism ideology, leadership and political organisations seen as "safe" for imperialism.

The question then arises: What would Kenya have looked like if the democratic, radical forces fighting colonialism and imperialism had not been thwarted by imperialist machinations? Some military and political aspects of the War of Independence and Mau Mau, examined earlier, point to the type of society they were aspiring to. It is important to put such glimpses into a fuller picture of what a society and government, guided by Mau Mau's vision, would have looked like had imperialism not disrupted the natural development of society in Kenya. While, by its very nature, such an endeavour has to be speculative as the process was not allowed to reach fruition, there is enough evidence to indicate what type of society would have emerged under Mau Mau. The recently released colonial files, more primary research on Mau Mau and a careful study of material already in the public domain would, perhaps, build up a fuller picture. It is for this reason, among others, that there is an urgent need to set up a Mau Mau Research and Documentation Centre which could provide answers to the above question.

All that is possible within the scope of this book is to provide a brief glimpse into what Mau Mau and the War of Independence's policies, practices and vision could possibly have evolved into if they had not been scuppered by imperialism and its local allies in Kenya.

Among the social fabric that colonialism destroyed, using the excuse of the Emergency, was the civic society painstakingly developed by Kenyans. Millner (1954?) mentions some early developments at political and social levels that would have continued into and beyond independence had they not been disrupted by Britain, whose aim, far from "civilising the natives", was to make people materially and mentally dependent on colonialism forever.

In order to press their modest and reasonable demands - the African's land hunger, wages questions, education, health services, colour bar and the constitutional issue - the Africans created their own political party - the Kenya African Union, which by 1952 had a membership of 100,000.

> To assist them in their struggle for better terms of employment African workers formed trade unions, the most important of which was the Labour Trade Union of East Africa; and in 1949 they formed the East African Trade Union Congress.

> To meet their thirst and longing for education they built their own schools and set up educational associations. By the end of 1952 there were nearly 200 African independent schools which had been organised by two bodies known as Kikuyu Independent Schools' Association and the Kikuyu Karing'a Educational Association.

> Africans published their own newspapers and other printed material in order that their wishes and needs could be publicly expressed.

> *Every one of these ordinary democratic activities were crushed by the British rulers of Kenya* by means of a Series of laws, apparently intended to completely stifle the expression of grievances of the African and deny him any and every form of association and organisation which could help him in his struggle. [italics added].

Gachihi (1986) provides a good analysis of the role played by independent schools and the reasons the colonial government closed them down:

> Young boys and girls were recruited from the ranks of the Independent Schools that were managed by the Kikuyu Independent Schools Association, a factor that led to the closure by Government order of thirty one such schools on 19th November, 1953.

This was an attempt to attack those aspects that had the potential to create a democratic society based on principles of justice and equality after independence. Had these achievements been allowed to survive and develop, they would certainly have been part of a future government, possibly led by a Mau Mau Party. But the colonial practice was to eliminate entire nations as in USA and Australia, chop off fingers, thumbs and hands of skilled workers - as in India as shown by Tharoor (2016) - or to force-feed people with opium - as in China - so as to ensure that the achievements of people were destroyed and then render them powerless and dependent on imperialism for their lives and livelihood.

Mwakenya (1987a) sums up the failed attempts for democratic opposition to the neo-colonial situation that was supported by the comprador KANU party:

> Organised resistance against neo-colonial rule started with organisations like KKM (Kiama Kia Muingi), which after realising the neo-colonial betrayal, attempted to regroup ex-freedom fighters to continue fighting for their land and freedom. This organisation was ruthlessly suppressed and many of its members brutally murdered by the new KANU regime. It took our people less than three years after the flag independence to organise an opposition political party. K. P. U. (Kenya Peoples Union), formed in 1966. It was a legal opposition party which advocated land reform and some socialist plicies in Kenya. The ruling neo-colonial regime banned K. P. U. in 1969, and massacred and ruthlessly repressed its members and supporters. Leaders like Oginga Odinga were detained without trial and others like Bildad Kaggia silenced.

> Although there were various types of resistance including armed struggle by Mau Mau, some of whom had returned to the mountains, and by N.P.P. in the North, the democratic resistance in this period 1963 - 1970 was typified by K.P.U. K.P.U. took the standpoint of the betrayed masses of the entire Kenya and advocated disengagement from foreign domination as the only basis of real economic take-off. It also advocated the socialist path of development. K.P.U. was the genuine inheritor and continuation of radical nationalism in Kenya.

It was, however, clear that the KANU government would allow no democratic expression and feared facing KPU in a fair general election.

Trade Unions

It was seen earlier that it was the radical trade union organisations which had injected working class ideology and leadership into the liberation struggle. As Durrani (2015a) points out:

> The working class, organised around trade union movements, played a critical role in the struggle for independence as well as in achieving the rights of working people.

Both these forces, imperialism and the neo-colonial regimes in Kenya, saw the liberation movement as a whole and the trade union movement as threats to their minority rules. Millner (1954?) explains further the reasons for attacks on the trade union movement:

> The trade union movement has been subjected to a Series of attacks, over a number of years, calculated to remove all independence of thought and action and render it totally impotent.

> Trade union leaders were arrested and deported, and repressive legislation was passed, culminating in the Trade Union Ordinance, 1952, which placed the trade unions under strict control of the Government. Introduced the infamous system of "probationary" trade unions and contained elaborate provisions intended to encourage the creation of docile "employees' associations" in place of genuine trade unions.

It is clear that had a Mau Mau government come to power, it would have championed the cause of the working class and its organisation, the trade unions. This could have checked or prevented the wholesale sell-out of national wealth to comprador and corporations and prevented the continued exploitation of labour.

Democracy

Besides the various Mau Mau documents that indicate the movement's approach to democracy, there is evidence in many reports from activists about the democratic practices that were invoked whenever Mau Mau were in control of small or large groups of people. It should, however, be noted that the conditions created by colonialism and its constant attacks under which Mau Mau operated were harsh and yet even under these situations, democracy prevailed. An example is that of Mau Mau democratic practices in the way it was organised nationally, as well as in concentration/detention centres. Barnett and Njama (1966) provide evidence of the former. Mathu (1974) shows the organisation and democracy even at Athi River Detention camp:

> Within each compound a leader was elected to represent the detainees in dealing with the camp commander. In the hardcore compounds men were chosen for their loyalty to the Movement and ability to speak English.

> Apart from this elected leader we had a secret organization within the four hardcore compounds. It was organized by grouping the men within each compound according to their location, division and district. In each compound there were committees representing the three Kikuyu districts plus Embu and Meru. At the top was a central committee of members from each compound and district. A system was set up in which notes, written on scraps of paper, were passed between leaders of the compounds. Where a decision had to be reached by the central committee, notes were wrapped around a stone and thrown from compound to compound. Each member would indicate his agreement with what had already been written or add his own ideas. This continued until a unanimous decision was reached... A number of rules existed... elders and disabled men had to be respected and given easy jobs...

Similarly, Muchai (1973) provides another example of Mau Mau organisation and democracy in the forest even as the "repressive measures of [the British Colonial] Government increased":

> In June 1953 a new Kiambu District Committee was formed. It consisted of 24 members who stayed in the Limuru European-settled area. I was elected with another man from my location to represent Kiambaa. Two members were elected from each of the three division committees and from each of Kiambu's nine locations. Our people in Nairobi also sent two members to attend important meetings.

While the appointments made in the forest for over-all Mau Mau posts such as those for the Kenya Parliament were based on elections, sometimes involving thousands of participants, the same was the case at even at the lowest and local levels: such appointments were made by elections. This contrasts with the British practice of rule by appointing District Commissioners and Chiefs who were given powers including that of confiscating property and passing and carrying out death sentences. And Muchai (1973) records, the Mau Mau practice was to elect committees and spokesmen. "We also elected cooks and allocated the various jobs involved in cleaning up and maintaining the camp", he adds. Surely it was the British who needed a lesson on democracy from the Kenyan resistance movement.

Millner (1954?) points out that "under the 'Emergency' the Governor has power (over and above the powers of the Council of Ministers) to make laws by decree, and he has been given the assistance of a War Council". It is these illegal and arbitrary powers that colonialism had given itself that were used to suppress the achievements of Mau Mau and earlier resistance movements.

The various declarations and statements from Mau Mau , including the document "The Struggle for Kenya's Future" and others reproduced in Appendix B gave a clear picture of the type of society that would have emerged under a progressive agenda supported by Mau Mau. That this aspect has not been explored fully is an indication of the control over information and communication that has been imposed on Kenyan minds by imperialism and their comprador agents in Kenya.

End the Conspiracy of Silence

Perhaps the greatest difficulty faced by Mau Mau veterans and those who even today support its aims is the lack of correct information among the public about the movement, its leadership, its vision and action. This is highlighted by a number of people who have in-depth knowledge about the movement. They say:

Our plea to break the conspiracy of silence about the Kenya Land and Freedom Army struggle includes also a plea for a more serious study of the history of Kenya since the Second World War and more particularly since 1952.[42]

It is only in recent years that this conspiracy is being challenged as new material, interpretations and analyses of the movement become available. But biographies and other historical records by Kenyan historians and Mau Mau activists have existed over a long period – easily ignored by those seeking to suppress the reality of atrocities.

Breaking the silence will reveal truth about British colonialism all over the world as highlighted by Tharoor (2016a):

> "You cannot quantify the wrongs done," he told the PTI news agency. The dehumanisation of Africans and the Caribbeans, the (mass) of psychological damage, the undermining of social traditions, our property rights, authority structures of these societies all in the interest of British colonialism. The fact remains that many of today's problems in these countries, including the persistence - in some cases the creation – of racial, ethnic and religious tensions were the direct result of colonialism.. There is a moral debt to be paid.

It is only those guilty of stealing and those continuing to benefit from the theft of national wealth who would oppose breaking the silence. Unfortunately, they are in positions of power - both nationally and internationally - and so would rather imprison history than let the full light of truth shine on historical facts.

It is not only the silence about history that imperialism has imposed in Kenya that needs to be dismantled. A society based on wealth and power for a minority elite needs to be attacked and a new social order created that ensures justice and equality for the majority of people. That is the challenge in Kenya today as much as it is in Britain.

---

42 The plea is made by Bildad Kaggia, Fred Kubai, Joseph Murumbi, and Achieng Oneko. See Barnett, Donald and Njama, Karari (1966): op. cit. Preface. p. ii.

Colonialism does not end on the day of independence, as if it was a switch to turn a light on or off. The attitudes, power-relations, classes and class struggles from the past are carried on into the future unless there has been a thoroughgoing revolution which alone can replace capitalism with socialism. This certainly did not happen in Kenya. Bolivian President Evo Morales established a Vice Ministry of Decolonization to address this issue. The Vice Minister Felix Cardenas is quoted by *Lessons from Latin America on Fighting Colonialism* (2016):

> It's not sufficient to go somewhere and say, 'I declare you decolonized!' and that's it, they're decolonized. No. It's a question of changing mentality, behaviour, of life philosophy, and to do this at an individual level, or at a communitarian level, a national level, we have an obligation to first ask 'what is Bolivia?' If we don't clearly understand what Bolivia is, then we don't know what needs to be done.

In the case of Kenya, the question, "What is Kenya?" needs to be answered by understanding its history of colonialism, by making a class analysis of its people, by examining class struggles and by examining the impact and activities of foreign governments and corporations in exploiting the country and influencing government policies. The question also needs to be answered by knowing on behalf of which class are government policies, the mass media, the education system and other social institutions run. And all this needs to be seen in the context of the way imperialism affects not only Kenya, but the entire continent of Africa. The context for the imperialist exploitation of Africa, for example, is given by *Honest Accounts* (2017):

> Much more wealth is leaving the world's most impoverished continent than is entering it, according to new research into total financial flows into and out of Africa. The study finds that African countries receive $161.6 billion in resources such as loans, remittances and aid each year, but lose $203 billion through factors including tax avoidance, debt payments and resource extraction, creating an annual net financial deficit of over $40 billion.

The only way to address such massive exploitation of "independent" Africa is through a well organised, united, Africa-wide resistance movement guided by anti-imperialist ideology. One of the reasons that imperialism invaded Libya leading to the murder of Muammar Gaddafi was that he had the vision and the resources to develop an anti-imperialist Africa. Earlier murders of Patrice Lumumba and the overthrow of Kwame Nkrumah were not enough to silence Africa's demand for liberation from imperialism.

British colonialism in Kenya was resisted by all nationalists. It would be strange if the resistance was then not continued after independence in the neo-colonial stage. The War of Independence had broader aims than just the achievement of independence. The struggle for liberation thus continued after independence as these aims had been subverted by colonialism in alliance with the newly created local elites. The context is set by Umoja Co-ordinator (1987):

> The route to real changes in Africa is not through coup d'états, whether progressive or not, but through the liberation forces completely rooted in the people. Power to the people has to mean a people's armed forces that would defend real changes which would liberate our economy, our politics, and our culture from neo-colonial control. The organised power of the alliance of the working class and the peasantry is the only basis of real changes. This is something that cannot come about simply by itself or spontaneously or through pious words and correct slogans - it is a goal to be worked for deliberately and consciously.

And that was the route taken by various progressive organisations, including Mau Mau, in the War of Independence. And that was also the route taken by people *after* independence.

The future of independent Kenya was charted by the departing colonial government by ensuring that the new government would follow a pro-capitalist, pro-imperialist path. And in deepening internal divisions along class lines in terms of wealth, income and property, it also set fertile grounds for resistance to the new government's policies. Anderson (2016) sums up the scenario clearly:

> At Kenya's independence in 1963, following the suppression of the rebellion, it was the loyalists who claimed the political victory and filled the ranks of the new African government. In a critical move that was intended first to ensure victory in the counter-insurgency war, the British

made a bargain with their African loyalist allies that involved agreement over the safe surrender of Mau Mau fighters, and that gave amnesty and impunity from prosecution for both rebels and loyalist militia.

… British commitment to their loyalist allies was such that they could not conceive of how to govern Kenya without them. Despite the noise made by European Settlers over the precipitous British decision to 'scuttle and run' from Kenya after 1959, it was the Kikuyu loyalists, and not the white highlanders, whose interests the departing colonialists would work hard to secure: white Settlers were expendable, Kikuyu loyalist allies were not.

It should be noted that Britain managed to gain the support of loyalists by means of bribery, looting, corruption and killing. It thereby legitimised the use of such methods for the in-coming government of Kenya. And, interestingly, it did not use British resources to achieve its aims. It was the land of Kenyan peasants, the labour of Kenyan workers, it was the resources of Kenyan people that were allowed to be looted so that a government loyal to neo-colonialism could be placed in position of power. It was a cheap bargain for imperialism. It had developed this method of using colonies' own resources for colonial plunder from its practice in India, among other places. What Tharoor (2016) says in relation to India and British colonialism, applies equally to the case of Kenya and British colonialism. "We literally paid for our own oppression", he says. The legacy of lasting poverty and landlessness affects Kenyan working people to this day. And in the same way, the legacy of killing, jailing, torture and massacres that Britain passed on to independent Kenya is happily endorsed by the successors of the loyalist government but this time using Kenyan armed forces to suppress and subdue people. Britain is quietly out of the picture, happily enjoying the fruits of its neo-colonial policies.

That the legacy of resistance to oppression and exploitation by British colonialism has continued in independent Kenya is not a matter of surprise. It was the conditions created by capitalism that created resistance to it. Those conditions have not changed and they have had everlasting consequences on the lives of the people.

References and Bibliography

Alam, S.M. Shamsul (2007): Rethinking Mau Mau in Colonial Kenya. New York, Palgrave Macmillan.

Alam, S. M. Shamsul and Gachihi, Margaret (2007): Women and Mau Mau. Chapter in Alam, S.M.S.(2007).

Anderson, David M. (2016): Making the Loyalist Bargain: Surrender, Amnesty and Impunity in Kenya's Decolonization, 1952–63. *The International History Review*. pp. 48-70. Published online: 19 Sep 2016. Available at: http://www.tandfonline.com/doi/full/10.1080/07075332.20 16.1230769 [Accessed: 09-06-17].

Angelo, Anaïs (2017): Jomo Kenyatta and the Repression of the 'Last' Mau Mau Leaders, 1961–1965. *Journal of Eastern African Studies*. Vol.11, No. 3, pp.442-459.

Barnett, Donald L. and Njama, Karari (1966): Mau Mau from Within: Autobiography and Analysis of Kenya's Peasant Revolt. New York: Monthly Review Press.

Barton, Frank. (1979): The Press in Africa: Persecution and Perseverance". New York: Africana Publication Co.

Brecht, Bertolt (1935): Questions From a Worker Who Reads. Available at: https://www.marxists.org/subject/art/literature/brecht/ [Accessed: 01- 06-17].

Bufacchi, Vittorio (2017): Colonialism, Injustice and Arbitrariness. *Journal of Eastern African Studies* Vol. 8 (4).

Buijtenhuijs, Rob ((1982): Essays on Mau Mau: Contributions to Mau Mau Historiography. Leiden: African Studies Centre. Research Report no. 17.

Clayton, Anthony and Donald C. Savage (1974): Government and Labour in

Kenya, 1895-1963. London: Routledge. 2016 print.

Corfield, F. D. (1960): Historical Survey of the Origin and Growth of Mau Mau. Cmd. 1030. London: HMSO.

Cushion, Steve (2016): A Hidden History of the Cuban Revolution: How the Working Class Shaped the Guerrilla Victory. New York: Monthly Review Press.

Dowden, Richard (2005): State of Shame. *The Guardian.* 05-02- 2005. Available at: www.guardian.co.uk/books/2005/feb/05/featuresreviews. guardianreview6 [Accessed: 24-04-17].

Durrani, Nazmi (2017): Jaswant Singh Bharaj. *In*: Durrani, Nazmi, Naila Durrani and Eddie Pereira (2017).

Durrani, Shiraz (2006): Never Be Silent: Publishing and Imperialism in Kenya, 1884-1963. London-Nairobi: Vita Books.

Durrani, Shiraz (2015b): Reflections on the Revolutionary Legacy of Makhan Singh. *In*: Durrani, Shiraz (2015) Ed.: Makhan Singh.

Durrani, Shiraz (2018): Kenya's War of Independence: Mau Mau and its Legacy of Resistance to Colonialism and Imperialism, 1948-1990. Nairobi: Vita Books.

Durrani, Shiraz (forthcoming): Pio Gama Pinto: The Assassinated Hero of the Anti-Imperialist Struggle in Kenya, 1927-1965. *In:* Durrani, Shiraz (Ed.): Pio Gama Pinto, the Assassinated Hero of the Anti-Imperialist Struggle in Kenya, 1927-1965.

Edgerton, Robert B. (1990): Mau Mau, An African Crucible. London: I.B.Tauris.

Every Leader Who Has Stood Up For Africa's Right To Economic Self-determination Has Been Eliminated. *in How Africa.* Available at: http://

howafrica.com/every-leaders-who-has-stood-up-for-africas-right-to-economic-self-determination-has-been-eliminated/#page. [Accessed: 08- 04- 17]

Furedi, Frank (1973): The African Crowd in Nairobi: Popular Movements and Elite Politics. Journal of African History. Vol. 2 (1973), pp. 275-290.

Furedi, Frank (1989): The Mau Mau War in Perspective. London: James Currey.

Gachihi, Margaret Wangui (1986): Role of Kikuyu Women in the Mau Mau (1986). MA Degree thesis. Nairobi: University of Nairobi.

Gatabaki, Njehu. (1983): "20   Great Years of Independence". Nairobi: Productions and Communications.

Great Britain. Colonial Of ce. Parliamentary Delegation to Kenya. Report (1954). Quoted in Barnett, Donald and Njama, Karari (1966): Mau Mau From Within. New York. Monthly Review.

History of Kenya, 1952-1958. (1976): A guide to the exhibition by Kenyan artists Mule wa Musembi, Kitonyi wa Kyongo, Kitaka wa Mutua and Mutunga wa Musembi held at Cottage Crafts, Nairobi in 1976. Publicity lea et. Exhibition organised by Sultan Somjee.

Honest Accounts 2017: How the world profits from Africa's wealth. Published by a coalition of UK and African organisations, including Global Justice Now, Health Poverty Action and Jubilee Debt Campaign. Available at: http://www.globaljustice.org.uk/sites/default/files/files/resources/honest_accounts_2017_web_final. pdf?utm_source=Global+Justice+Now+press+release+list&utm_ campaign=17a92094cc-EMAIL_CAMPAIGN_2017_05_17&utm_ medium=email&utm_term=0_166972fef5-17a92094cc- 288067141&mc_ cid=17a92094cc&mc_eid=6149d72169 [Accessed: 11- 06-17].

"Hunting The Mau Mau" under the sections British military strategy in Kenya; the RAF in Kenya; British units involved in the Emergency in Kenya. Available at: www.britains-smallwars.com/kenya/index.html [Accessed: 19-01-12].

Kabubi, Anna Wamuyu (2002): Interview, "A Fight of Her Own: Conversation with Anna Wamuyu Kabubi" [Mau Mau name, Cinda Reri]. "Women and Mau Mau", Interview by S. M. Shamsul and Margaret Gachihi. *in*:Alam (2007).

Kaggia, Bildad (1975): Roots of Freedom 1921–1963: The Autobiography of Bildad Kaggia. Nairobi: East African Publishing House.

Kaggia, Bildad, W. de Leeuw and M. Kaggia (2012): The Struggle for Freedom and Justice: The Life and Times of the Freedom Fighter and Politician Bildad M. Kaggia (1921-2005). Nairobi: Transafrica Press.

Kariuki, Josiah Mwangi (1975): Mau Mau Detainee: The Account of a Kenyan African of his Experiences in Detention Camps, 1953-1960. Nairobi: Oxford University Press.

Kasrils, Ronnie (2013): How the ANC's Faustian pact sold out South Africa's poorest. *The Guardian*. 24 June 2013. Available at: http://m. guardian. co.uk/commentisfree/2013/jun/24/anc-faustian-pact-mandela-   fatal-error [Accessed: 08-04-17]

Kenya Committee for Democratic Rights for Kenya (London). (1952-60): "Kenya Press Extracts". Photocopies of the Extracts available in the Kenya Liberation Library. The Committee was based at 86 Rochester Row, London. SW1.

Kinyatti, Maina wa (2008): History of Resistance in Kenya, 1884-2002. Nairobi: Mau Mau Research Centre. SEP

Kubai, Fred. (1983): The Struggle for Independence: Background to the nationalist movement. Gatabaki, Njehu (1983).

Leakey, L.S.B. (1954): Defeating Mau Mau. London: Methuen.

Leigh Day (2016): Historical Background. Available at: https://www. leighday. co.uk/International-and-group-claims/Kenya/The-Mau-Mau-   claims/ Historical-background-to-the-Mau-Mau-claims [Accessed: 14-11- 16].

Lessons from Latin America on Fighting Colonialism (2016). teleSUR, 23-04-2016. Available at: http://www.telesurtv.net/english/analysis/ Lessons-from-Latin-America-on-Fighting-Colonialism-20160423-0036. html. [Accessed: 24-05-17].

McGhie, John. (2002): "British Brutality in Mau Mau Conflict". The Guardian. (London). November 9, 2002.

Maina, Paul (1977): Six Mau Mau Generals. Nairobi: Gazelle Books.

Maloba, Wunyabari O. (1998): Mau Mau and Kenya: An Analysis of a Peasant Revolt. Oxford: James Currey.

Mathu, Mohamed (1974): The Urban Guerrilla. Life Histories from the Revolution No. 3. Richmond, B.C., Canada: LSM Information Centre.

Millner, Ralph (1954?): The Right to Live. London: The Kenya Committee.

Mirii, Ngugi wa (1979): On Literacy Content. Institute for Development Studies, University of Nairobi. Discussion Paper No. 340.

Muchai, Karigo (1973): The Hardcore. Life Histories from the Revolution No. 1. Richmond,B.C., Canada: LSM Information Centre.

Field Marshal Muthoni (2007): Conversations with A Freedom Fighter. Interview. Available at: http://wherehermadnessresides.blogspot. com/2005/09/conversations-with-freedom- ghter.html. [Accessed: 19- 04-2007].

Mwakenya (1987a): Draft Minimum Programme.

Newsinger, J. (2006): The Blood Never Dried: A People's History of the British Empire. London: Bookmarks.

Ngotho, Kamau (2008): Secret land deal that made Kenyatta First President. *Daily Nation*. 20-09-2008. Available at: http://www.nation.co.ke/news/-/1056/473158/-/5gb13cz/-/index.html [Accessed: 29-01-2017].

Odinga, Oginga (1968): Not Yet Uhuru. London. Heinemann.

Oneko, Ramogi Achieng (1966): Detention Days. *in Pio Gama Pinto, Independent Kenya's First Martyr - Socialist Freedom Fighter* (1966).

Pinto, Pio Gama (1963a): Glimpses of Kenya's Nationalist Struggle. *Pan Africa*. *Also published as a monograph*: Nowrojee, Viloo and Edward Miller (Editors, 2014): Glimpses of Kenya's Nationalist Struggle by Pio Gama Pinto. Nairobi: Asian African Heritage Trust.

Pio Gama Pinto, Independent Kenya's First Martyr - Socialist Freedom Fighter (1966). Nairobi: Pan African Press Ltd.

Quinn, Kate (2015): Foreword to Cushion, S. (2016).

Singh, Makhan (1969): History of Kenya's Trade Union Movement to 1952. Nairobi: East African Publishing House.

Singh, Makhan (1980): Kenya's Trade Unions: Crucial Years, 1952-56. Nairobi: Uzima Press.

Spencer, John (1983): James Beauttah: Freedom Fighter. Nairobi: Stellascope.

The Struggle For Kenya's Future. The document was written as "part of a collective effort by several Kenyans and myself [Don Barnett]...It was mimeographed and distributed at the Kenya African National Union (KANU) conference held in Nairobi, Kenya in December 1961" - Don Barnett in Muchai, K. (1973): 5-9.

Tamaduni Players, Nairobi. (1978). Publicity material.

Tharoor, Shashi (2016a): An Era of Darkness: The British Empire in India. New Delhi: Aleph.

Tharoor, Shashi (2016c): Does Britain Owe Reparations to India and Other Former Colonies? *South China Morning Post*. 4-12-16. Available at: http://www.scmp.com/week-asia/opinion/article/2050394/does-britain-owe-reparations-india-and-other-former-colonies [accessed: 30-06-17].

Thomsen, Lars Ulrika (2017): The Anniversary of Lenin's *Imperialism*. The *Communist Review*. No. 82. Winter 2016-2017.

Truth Justice and Reconciliation Commission of Kenya (2013) [TJRC]: Final Report. Available at http://digitalcommons.law.seattleu.edu/tjrc/ [Accessed: 08-04-17]. Vol.IIA.

Umoja Co-ordinator (1987): Progressive Forces Must Unite For a New Kenya. Statement from the Co-ordinator at the Unity Conference of Patriotic, Democratic and Progressive Kenyan Organisations Abroad. London, October 16-19.

Venys, Ladislav (1970): A History of the Mau Mau Movement in Kenya. Department of Asian and African Studies, Faculty of Philosophy. Prague: Charles University.

Wasserman, Gary (1976): Politics of Decolonization: Kenya Europeans and the Land Issue, 1960–1965. Cambridge: Cambridge University Press.

PART 2

Ed., Julie MaCarthur, *Dedan Kimathi on Trial:* Colonial Justice and Popular Memory in Kenya's Mau Mau Rebellion (Athens, Ohio: Ohio University Press, 2017) 406 pages +xxv

Review by Willy Mutunga[43]

The Debates Shall Continue

This book produces Kimathi's entire trial proceedings, judgment, appeals, including the last one to the Privy Council. The Foreword is by Professors Micere Mugo and Ngugi wa Thiong'o. There are five critical essays about the trial and Kimathi's legacy, two by Kenyan Professors Simon Gikandi and Nicholas Kariuki Githuku. The other three are by historians who have researched and written on the history of Kenya for decades: John M Lonsdale, David Anderson, Julie Macarthur, and Lotte Hughes. Other prominent Kenyan historians are quoted in the book (Maina wa Kinyatti, Bethwell Allan Ogot, E.S. Atieno Adhimbo, John Nottingham, among

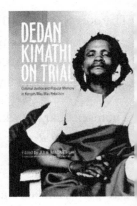

others). Literary writers also feature prominently in the critical essays. So do the writings of Mau Mau freedom fighters themselves .[44] There is no doubt this book is extremely rich as a resource on what has been written on Mau Mau in general and on Kimathi in particular. It is definitely going to be a compulsory reading for public and organic intellectuals, activists, and particularly the young Kenyans who yearn for a revolutionary change in their Motherland.

This book settles some of the debates that still rage on about Dedan Kimathi. We now know Kimathi was executed and buried in Kamiti Maximum Security Prison. We now have the complete colonial record of his trial. We have Professor Julie Macarthur to thank for "The Hunt for (the Trial of) Dedan Kimathi"[45] A copy of this record has now a pride of place in the Museum for the Judiciary. Other copies are in the custody of his widow, Mukami, at the Kenya National Archives, and with the Mau Mau Veteran's Association. The search for his

---

43   Former Chief Justice & President of the Supreme Court of Kenya.

44   See, for example, page 26, endnotes 2, 8, and 14. Another publication on the Mau Mau in 2017 is Shiraz Durrani's *Kenya's War of ndependence: Mau Mau and its Legacy of Resistance to Colonialism and Imperialism, 1948-1990* (London: Vita Books, 2017). The debates shall continue.

45   Julie Macarthur's essay, page 6

ains continues. It is our great hope that the search for Kimathi's remains will
successfully completed. We still yearn for his heroic burial at the Freedom
ner, Uhuru Park, Nairobi.[46]

ill not review the critical essays here, a task I leave to the readers. I warn
readers, however, that the volume is a great resource for the debates on
athi. Indeed, the volume will undeniably be yet another source of more
ates. Micere Mugo and Ngugi wa Thiong'o foretell this in their Foreword
e book:

> If the publication of colonial records, which are pitted against
> interpretive narratives of leading scholars on Kenya, including Kenyan
> intellectuals such as Simon Gikandi and Nicholas Githuku, as well as
> other international researchers on Kenya, helps reignite the debate about
> Kimathi's legacy to Kenya, Africa, and the world, it will have served a
> great purpose.[47]

onialist and Imperialist Injustice vs Jurisprudence of Liberation Anderson
is critical essay gives us a glimpse of this injustice when he writes about the
cial Emergency Assizes. Kimathi was tried by one of them:

> To appreciate how the [Kimathi] trial was conducted it is first important
> to understand that although the Special Emergency Assizes were a
> division of the Supreme Court and heard capital cases, they functioned
> in a radically different way from that normally expected in a courtroom
> under British jurisdiction. These assize courts offered a stripped-down
> and truncated version of "British justice," with the legal practicalities
> specifically shaped to the circumstances of a colonial war of insurrection.

Why has this issue not been resolved? In the 1960s one would guess both the Kenyan and British
rnments did not want the issue resolved for political reasons: the land question had not been resolved;
pposition would have been seen to win if the issue was resolved; and this was still in the Cold War with
ological and political debates. *(See William Attwood, The Reds and the Blacks, A Personal Adventure
')*. 55 years since independence, the Mau Mau Veterans' Association exists and its ban was lifted by the
an NARC government of 2002-7; Kimathi has been glorified in a statue in the Central Business District
irobi; and in the naming of schools and institutes after him; the British have apologized for the tortures
committed in the country during the Mau Mau War of Independence, and indeed, built a monument in
u Park to atone for their imperialist sins. So why is the heroic burial of Kimathi such a great political
em for the two governments? I refuse to believe that both governments do not know where the remains
mathi are. Is there still a great fear by both governments that a Kimathi Shrine in Nairobi would ignite
a's revolutionary spirit?

Page xvii. Indeed, there was a debate around Nicholas Githuku's critical essay that a critical
wer for the publishing press of the volume ignited. At some point in this debate Githuku threatened to
raw his critical essay from the volume.

It is a striking paradox of the Special Assize Courts that because they had been set up to deal specifically with Mau Mau crimes under the Emergency Powers there was seldom any attempt to establish the motive for the crime, even an act of murder, in the cases brought to trial. This avoided any discussion in court of the aims and objectives of Mau Mau as a movement, and so denied the accused any opportunity to present a political case. These cases are therefore all about Mau Mau, but Mau Mau is hardly ever mentioned in the proceedings.[48]

Professor Githuku argues:

Ultimately, instead of simply appreciating, literally, the black-and-white facts or demerits of the case against Kimathi, I seek, in the conclusion of this reflection and with the benefit of the hindsight, to argue that what's important is what is not on trial in this judicial process.[49]

...

...The entire trial and its findings were very much the product of the chaotic, emotionally charged, and racially volatile political situation of the Emergency period.[50]

The 2010 Constitution of Kenya has as one of its visions decolonizing of the colonial and neocolonial jurisprudence. The Constitution provides a theory of its interpretation to protect itself from the common law cannons of interpretation that allow judicial officers to bring in their intellectual, ideological, and political biases into the interpretation of cases, statutes, and the Constitution itself. The Kenyan Constitution is perhaps the only constitution in the world that provides for a theory of its interpretation. Reinforced by the provisions of the The Supreme Court Act, 2011 and a majority decision of the Supreme Court,[51] courts need not look beyond the Constitution to interpret it.[52] The Constitution decrees that judicial officers make law.[53]

---

48   Page 234
49   Page 287
50   Page 287-288
51   In what is now famously called the *Digital Migration Case*
52   "Human Rights States and Society Under Transformative Constitutions: Reflect from Kenya" in *Transnational Human Rights Review Vol 2 (December 2015), 63-102*; "The 2010 Constitution of Kenya and its Interpretation. Reflections from Supreme Court Decisions" in *Speculum Juris Vol 29 Part I 2015, 1*
53   Article 20 (3) (a) & (b) of the 2010 Constitution

e Supreme Court Act, 2011 provides for delving into history, sociology, nomics, philosophy, and other sources to interpret the provisions of the nstitution. Staunch positivism tells us to ignore these non-legal phenomena ause the law is the law is the law! Our Constitution does not countenance unch positivism.

e modern Bill of Rights in the 2010 Constitution decrees procedures and hts that would condemn the Kimathi trial for what it was, a gross injustice. e record of Kimathi's trial provides a great backdrop to the past the 2010 nstitution wanted ended and never to be repeated. Through the Bill of ghts and other pillars of the constitution (for example, equitable distribution reasons, the economic, social, cultural, and environmental rights) politics not be kept out of the courtrooms anymore. Indeed, there is a compelling ument that judiciaries are institutional political actors, particularly those that plement transformative constitutions.[54]

the Judiciary's blueprint for transformation, The Judiciary Transformation mework 2012-2016[55] ,one of the four pillars of that transformation is the use echnology as an enabler for justice. The judiciary has sought to do away with notes of judicial officers being the sole record of the court proceedings. While ceedings will be recorded verbatim a lot attention is also paid to translations. Judiciary saw clearly that leaving the recording of the proceedings to at judicial officers take down as the record could result in gross injustice ause of corruption besides the biases of the judicial officers. This volume, refore, provides the Judiciary and lawyers a great opportunity to critically ttinize the record of Kimathi's trial in view of this background on the theory nterpretation of the Constitution and the blueprint for transformation of the iciary. Such scrutiny is also about the integrity of the colonial and post-onial court proceedings. There are judicial officers that take notes of the ceedings in long hand in the Kenyan Judiciary.

the Judiciary, the legal profession, and the legal scholars the record of this l awaits a great debate on imperial and colonial injustice. What has and has not nged? How does our post-independence jurisprudence, and particularly the we are developing from the 2010 Constitution rescued the former? Students academics of law have a rich material from which many aspects of the

---

Mutunga, "Politics, the Media and independence of the Judiciary: A personal Reflection," A ure delivered for ACME, Uganda, Kampala, November 8, 2017; Human Rights States and Society, note

Nairobi: Kenya Judiciary, 2012.

Kenya Resist No. 1

research, study, practice, and critique of the law and justice can be undertaken. Talking of technology how will artificial intelligence help in ending injustice, and guaranteeing the independence of individual judicial officers? Judiciaries and legal professions need to engage this debate on artificial intelligence judges.

When are the Seeds of Counter-revolution Planted in the Mau Mau War of Independence?

Professor Lonsdale in his critical essay delves on this critical question that historians and political scientists, and other disciplines raise.[56] Professor Lonsdale correctly locates this question to cover all "stakeholders:" the British, the loyalists, the struggles within the Mau Mau Freedom fighters themselves. As the seeds of independence are planted so are the seeds of counter-revolution. Indeed, also planted are seeds of further resistance and struggles that Professor Githuku analyses.[57] Professors Mugo and Wa Thiong'o also weigh in on this issue in their Foreword to the book. In my opinion this is a critical issue that reflects on the debates on the legacy of Kimathi. Those of us who imagine freedom and emancipation cannot ignore class struggles in freedom movements, particularly when the enemy begins to make concessions to the struggles. The book gives us very rich material to think through this critical issue. It is possible to argue that the 2010 Constitution is a continuation of the counter-revolution of the Mau Mau War of Independence. It is also possible to see that Constitution as a victory of some of the ideas and ideals of the War. The discussion on the Constitution's limitations cannot be conducted in a vacuum of this earlier history. Indeed, in Kenya the narratives and counter-narratives of the status quo continue to play a centre stage as unity of opposites.

Kimathi's Legacy

While urging all Kenyans and other global citizens to read this book, and other Mau Mau texts, I wanted to mention a profound comment by Professor Gikandi. In his essay carried in Chapter 4 of the volume (*Dedan Kimathi: The Floating Signifier and the Missing Body*) at page 323 he writes:

> If Kimathi's life is not extraordinary, why does he stand out as the great symbol of the anticolonial revolt in Kenya? And why does he attract the interest of creative writers? From a historical   perspective, as the other essays in this volume vividly illustrate, Kimathi's symbolic power

56   Pages 270-278
57   Pages 292-308

is enhanced by the enemies who demonize him and the followers who adore him.

My reflection on this profound contribution by Professor Gikandi is as follows: He states Kimathi's legacy very persuasively. As we study our great hero Kimathi we need to draw from his strengths and weaknesses from the texts of his enemies and his glorifiers. In doing so I believe we will be stoking his living revolutionary spirit into an everlasting revolutionary fire by consolidating his strengths and rescuing his weakness. Indeed, Kimathi was a human being with strengths and weaknesses. I believe this may be a message we give to the youth as they read about Kimathi's revolutionary struggle. And, as they imagine our freedom and emancipation from imperialisms of the West and East.

Indeed, Professor Macarthur gives a similar advice. She states:

> This volume is the product of collective labor. It belongs not to any one contributor but to all those who pick it up, read its pages, engage in its sometimes fierce debates, and imagine from its contents their own Kimathis.[58]

Congratulations:

The last two sentences of the Foreword by Professors Mugo and Ngugi wa Thiong'o record great appreciation for this book in the following words:

> We thank and commend Julie MacArthur, her editors, and the publishers for making these important colonial records available for public scrutiny and for the very first time in history.
> Congratulations[59]

Let the "hunt" for the remains of Kimathi now begin in earnest. Let us consolidate his strengths and rescue his weaknesses as the struggle to liberate Kenya from the imperialism of the West and East continues.

---

58   page xxi
59   Pages xii-xvii
Kenya Resist No. 1

Vita Books Publications

INFORMATION AND
LIBERATION
by Shiraz Durrani
Vita Books, Kenya

KENYA'S WAR OF
INDEPENDENCE
by Shiraz Durrani
Vita Books, Kenya

LIBERATING MINDS,
RESTORING KENYAN
HISTORY
by Nazmi Durrani
Vita Books, Kenya

MAKHAN SINGH. A
REVOLUTIONARY KENYAN
TRADE UNIONIST
by Shiraz Durrani
Vita Books, Kenya

NEVER BE SILENT
by Shiraz Durrani
Vita Books, Kenya

PROGRESSIVE
LIBRARIANSHIP
by Shiraz Durrani

Forthcoming

Pio Gama Pinto, the Assassinated Hero of the Anti-Imperialist Struggle in Kenya, 1927 - 1965. Edited by Shiraz Durrani

Pio Gama Pinto was born in Kenya on March 31, 1927. He was assassinated in Nairobi on February 24, 1965. In his short life, he became a symbol of anti-imperialist struggles in Kenya as well as in Goa in India. He was actively involved with Mau Mau during Kenya's war of independence. He was detained by the British colonial authorise from 1954-59. His contribution to the struggle for liberation for working people spanned two continents - Africa and Asia. It covered two

phases of imperialism - colonialism in Kenya and Goa and neo-colonialism in Kenya after independence. His enemies saw no way of stopping the intense, lifelong struggle waged by Pinto except through an assassin's bullets. But his contribution, his ideas, and his ideals are remembered and upheld even today by le active in liberation struggles.

o in his own words

*a's Uhuru must not be transformed into freedom to exploit, or freedom to
ungry and live in ignorance. Uhuru must be Uhuru for the masses – Uhuru
exploitation, from ignorance, disease and poverty (Pinto 1963).*
o was assassinated by the regime on 24 February 1965 and Kenya has yet
place him - Donald Barnett (1972).

*Pinto fell on the battlefield in our common war against neo-colonialism.
g with the immortal Patrice Lumumba ... he has joined the ranks of our
'yrs whose blood must be avenged. In such honourable company, his death
recruit new armies of Pintos to continue the fight in which he died [in] the
't to create a united socialist Africa - John K. Tettegah. (1966)*

N: 978-1-869886-04-2

IAct Ukombozi Library

Progressive African Library and Information Activists' Group (PALIAct)
ap the PALIAct Ukombozi Library, in partnership with Vita Books and
Mau Mau Research Centre in Nairobi in 2017. The Library aims to make
lable progressive material and to encourage reading, study and research by
cing people in Kenya.

need for such a library follows from the fact that progressive literature has
generally ignored by most libraries and learning institutions. Young people
passion to bring about improvement in the country and thirsty for materials
would inspire them in their quest for social justice get disappointed as such
rials are hard to come by.

Ukombozi Library has an initial collection of almost a thousand titles of
ressive material, mostly books but also pamphlets, videos and photographs.
corporates December Twelve Movement's underground library set up by

Nazmi Durrani in the 1980s. A majority of these are classics which are either out of print or cannot be found in the local bookshops. Other material has been donated by Mau Mau Research Centre, Vita Books and many progressive individuals active in the information struggle in Kenya.

Membership is open to all who agree with the vision and principles of the library, irrespective of class, ethnicity, religion, gender, region, race or disability. Individuals or institutional membership is available on payment of appropriate fees.

Further information can be obtained from
Progressive African Library and Information Activists (Paliact)
Second Floor, University Way Building Next to Lilian Towers Hotel
P.O Box 746-00200
Nairobi
Email: info.paliact17@gmail.com
Website: http://vitabooks.co.uk/projects-for-change/paliact/

Kenya Resists

Vita Books announces the Launch of a new series for 2018

Vita Books is pleased to announce the launch of a new series of handbooks under the title, *Kenya Resists*. The series covers different aspects of the resistance by people of Kenya to colonialism and imperialism. The handbooks are reproduced from published books, unpublished reports, research and oral or visual testimonies.

The series aims to provide an insight into the history of resistance by people of Kenya. Each number focuses on a specific aspect of resistance before and after independence. The first titles in the series has been taken from Shiraz Durrani's book, *Kenya's War of Independence, Mau Mau and its Legacy of Resistance to Colonialism and Imperialism, 1948-1990* (Nairobi: Vita Books) and from additional sources. The first 3 titles to be published in 2018 in the series are:

> **No. 1: Mau Mau, the Revolutionary Force from Kenya Challenges Colonialism and Imperialism, 1948-63.**

> **No. 2. Trade Unions and Kenya's War of Independence. Includes Reflections on Makhan Singh.**

> **No. 3: People's Resistance to Colonialism and Imperialism in Kenya. Includes presentations on Karimi Nduthu.**

  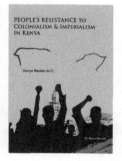

P.O. Box 62501-00200
Nairobi. Kenya
http://vitabooks.co.uk
info.vitabkske@gmail.com

Distributed Worldwide by: African Books Collective
Oxford, OX1 9EN
http://www.africanbookscollective.com/

Kenya Resist No. 1

Printed in the United States
By Bookmasters